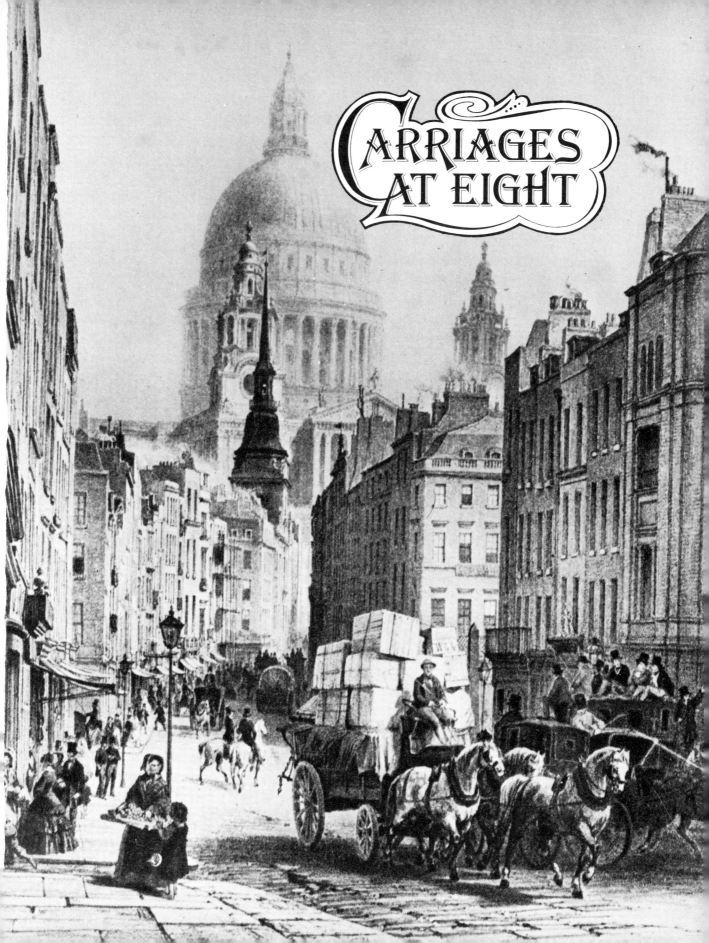

CARRIAGES AT EIGHT

LUTTERWORTH PRESS

Horse-drawn society in Victorian and Edwardian times
FRANK E. HUGGETT

First published 1979

Acknowledgements

Although numerous books have been published recently on Victorian carriages, there has never been a book about the people who rode in them, the men who drove them, and all the other servants, dealers, tradesmen and manufacturers who were needed to sustain this distinctive world. My journeys through times past to this previously unmapped period of history have been simplified by the generous assistance and the kind advice I have received from a large number of individuals, institutions and libraries. I am particularly grateful to the following for the special help they have given me: Mr. E. H. August; Mr. Robert Barley; Berkshire Record Office; the British Driving Society; The British Library, State Paper Room; Prof. Hugh Cockerell; East Sussex Record Office; Hampshire District Library headquarters, Southampton; Mr. C. R. Hannis; Huntingdon County Record Office; Leeds Library Services, Archives Department; the London Library; National Library of Wales, Department of Manuscripts and Records; Nottingham County Library, Local Studies Section; Royal Commission on Historical Manuscripts; Royal Society for the Prevention of Cruelty to Animals; West Sussex Record Office. They, of course, are in no way responsible for the facts or the opinions expressed in this book.

FEH

The illustration on the half-title shows St. Paul's from Ludgate Hill, London.

The illustration on the title page shows Hyde Park Corner 1821 by Henry Alken.

ISBN 0 7188 2351 6

COPYRIGHT © FRANK HUGGETT 1979

Filmset in Baskerville 12 on 15 pt: Quotes, 11 on 13 pt: Captions, 11 on 13 pt.

Set, printed and bound in Great Britain by
Fakenham Press Limited, Fakenham, Norfolk

CONTENTS

1

THE HORSE AND CARRIAGE AGE

One of the most sumptuous assemblies of coaches and carriages ever seen in England occurred on May 1, 1851, at the opening of the Great Exhibition in Hyde Park. Squires and country gentlemen had emerged from their homes in the depths of the English countryside to travel up to London in the traditional way in their heavy, lumbering family coaches, emblazoned with their crests and armorial bearings, and drawn by their most expensive horses in their heaviest and most flamboyant harness. The coachmen wore their smartest livery and the footmen rode on the platform at the back. Owing to the huge crowds of foreign and provincial visitors in London and the shortage of hotel accommodation, many of these country gentlefolk and their wives had to spend the night in their vehicles, emerging cramped, aching and somewhat irritable in the early hours of the morning to breakfast in a most unusual way. One Victorian lady, walking with her husband through Berkeley Square at 6 a.m. to see the sights on that great and exciting day, was astonished to find servants, many of them wearing powdered wigs, busily engaged in cooking bacon, boiling eggs and making tea on the pavement. "There was a great clattering of pots and pans and crockery," she recalled, "and a perfect babel of voices. Servants were shouting to each other and being shouted at in turn by their masters and mistresses; frail forms in silken gowns and richly-fashioned poke bonnets, with plaintive voices, were crying out for something hot to drink, and whilst distracted footmen were colliding with each other in their frantic efforts to be quick, we heard on all sides, 'Oh, do make haste, James', 'Do tell him to make haste, John', 'I am dying for a cup of tea, I shall faint if

(Left) *Oxford Circus at the height of the horse and carriage age.*

it isn't ready soon', and in gruffer tones, 'Come hurry up at once, James, or take a month's notice'."[1]

After breakfast, the squires were driven off to Hyde Park where their coaches were joined later by the smart new carriages and town coaches of the residents of the fashionable squares in which they had spent the night. By the time the exhibition had closed for the day, no less than 1,000 state coaches, 800 broughams, 600 post chaises, 300 clarences, 300 carriages of other kinds, and 1,500 cabs had entered the park. It was estimated that the vehicles would have stretched for twenty miles placed end to end.

This was the last occasion on which a large number of coaches were used for long-distance travel in Britain. Twenty years before, when railways were still in their infancy, wealthy lords usually travelled up to London in their post chaises or travelling chariots, the aristocratic equivalents of the stagecoach, which stopped every ten to twenty miles at a posting inn to engage fresh horses and new postboys. These tough little men, similar in build to a modern flat-race jockey, did not drive from the coachman's box, but as postilions, mounted on one of a pair of horses, with an iron guard strapped to their right leg to prevent it from being crushed between the horse they were riding and the pole. The usual charge was one shilling and sixpence a mile for a pair of horses and threepence to sixpence a mile for each postboy, a princely price in those days so that you needed to be a wealthy man to indulge in this form of private transport. When aristocrats went on Continental tours they travelled in a britzska or a dormeuse with an extended boot which could be converted into a bed. These coaches were equipped with everything that my lord or my lady might need in foreign parts, including sword cases, folding sunshades, Venetian blinds, interior lamps and hat boxes. Some of them were marvels of mechanical ingenuity like the one used by the fourth Lord Vernon, whom Charles Dickens encountered in Switzerland in 1846. "It was", Dickens wrote, "an extraordinary carriage, where you touch a spring and a chair flies out, touch another spring and a bed appears, touch another spring and a closet of pickles opens, touch another spring and disclose a pantry."[2]

By the 1850s the railways had brought the age of long-distance coaching to an end, except in some remote parts of the country. The great highways lay neglected and abandoned, with grass slowly reclaiming the verges. The roads were used only by "agricultural wagons, coal, stone and brick carts, brewers' drays, an occasional carriage, a few dog carts driven by gentlemen or farmers, and a sprinkling of village carts".[3] The old stage and mail coaches were sold off for scrap, though in the late Sixties a handful of coach-loving aristocrats reintroduced a limited service

8

The brougham was one of the most popular carriages in the Victorian age among both aristocrats and the middle classes.

on a few routes in the Home Counties; and aristocratic chariots (always pronounced "charrots" by ladies of fashion) were allowed to rot unused in a barn or a coach house in country stables, or were sold for a few pounds to a coachbuilder. Aristocrats started to make long journeys by train like everyone else, though in the early days, at least, they sometimes had their own private, crested railway carriage attached to an ordinary train, with a top-hatted footman sitting on a rumble seat outside.

There were many fears that the days of the horse-drawn vehicle were numbered; but, instead, the railways produced just as great a revolution in city streets as they had done on the great country highways. In 1833, just before Queen Victoria came to the throne, it was estimated that only $3\frac{1}{2}$m. people travelled from one city to another every *year*; only thirty years later the number of railway travellers had reached an annual total of 204m., an increase, even allowing for the growth in population, of forty times.[4] There was a similar great increase in freight traffic. But modern technology stopped at the rail termini – those vast memorials, engineered in iron and glass, of the Victorian age – where passengers had to step back in time

to the horse and carriage and where the greatly increased quantities of manufac-
tured goods had to be taken away by cart and wagon.

To cope with this great rise in inter-city traffic, more and more horses were
needed in the cities and the towns, so that before the end of the reign it needed
"over 300,000 living horse power to move the wheels along the roads of London".
Yet that was less than one-tenth of the total number of horses in the whole
country.[5] The city streets became choked, particularly in the rush hours, with a
straining, stamping, neighing mass of horseflesh, almost inextricably entangled at
various angles; while the air became so heavily polluted that one witness at an
official inquiry described the streets of London as "smelling of dung like a
stableyard".[6] As early as 1866, a writer in *Chamber's Journal* was already complaining that "Everybody's Carriage Stops the way":

> Yes, everybody's carriage stops the way. The omnibuses bringing city-men to
> business are reduced to an alternation of crawls and stand-still by the time they reach
> the city margin. The Hansom cabs can only go ahead by getting entangled among the
> four-wheelers, and endangering the lives of Materfamilias and the little ones. The
> private carriages of aldermen and well-to-do cits, when they venture east of Temple
> Bar, are in imminent danger of having their glossy panels burst in. The coal-wagons,
> brewers' drays, dock-wagons and sugar-wagons block the way, and are blocked;
> although *they* don't care, for nothing can hurt them. The hop-wagons threaten to hurl
> their bags and packets into the first-floor windows; while the timber-wagons are
> always ready to dash into the plate-glass shop windows. Pickford is ever quarrelling
> with Chaplin and Horne, as to which did not get out of the way when the other was
> coming. Butchers' and poulterers' carts at Leadenhall and Newgate Streets keep all
> other carts in defiance; while fishmongers' carts effectually blockade Lower Thames
> Street.[7]

Much of this urban horse-drawn transport was used for practical purposes,
carrying goods of all kinds and sizes to and from the railway stations, taking
commercial travellers with their samples and wares to suburban shops in the
rapidly expanding cities, and bringing middle-class commuters to work. But there
was another reason for the increase. For many centuries the ownership of a private
coach or carriage had been one of the main outward symbols of wealth, rank and
privilege. With the great increase in wealth and snobbery in the status-conscious
Victorian age, everyone who was anyone wanted to own a carriage or, at least, to
have the use of one. A carriage was a public proof of social success. As Thackeray,
that perceptive observer of Victorian snobbery, made the young George Osborne
haughtily proclaim in *Vanity Fair*: "My father's a gentleman, and keeps his
carriage."

Hyde Park was the venue for meetings of the aristocratic Four-in-Hand Club.
A painting by James Pollard, 1838.

Wealthy aristocrats needed seven or eight carriages to preserve their distinction from the rising middle classes and to provide a suitable vehicle for every aspect of their busy social life; professional men needed a carriage for themselves and another for their wives; middle-class ladies of humble origins wanted to drive out in a carriage in the afternoons to impress their friends and neighbours; young men needed a carriage to interest young ladies; and even the servants in big houses wanted to have the unauthorized use of a carriage, when the family was out of town, to take their kitchen guests back to other basements. There was a truly phenomenal rise in the number of private carriages in the nineteenth century from 60,000 in 1814, to 250,000 by 1860 and to 500,000 by 1901. At a time when the number of male indoor servants was falling, and haughty butlers were also being forced to take on the duties of a valet in some households or even (indignity of

*Members of London society loved to show off their grace and affluence in Rotten Row,
Hyde Park.*

indignities) being themselves replaced by cheaper parlourmaids, the total number
of private coachmen and grooms continued to increase, trebling in the last half of
the century.

A carriage, particularly a lady's carriage, was not so much a means of transport
but far more a way of life. The more expensive the horses and the carriage, the less
they were used. No first-rate carriage horse was expected to travel more than
fourteen miles a day at a maximum speed of 9 to 10 m.p.h., which was well below
its maximum range and speed. In the wealthiest establishments, a large, expensive
retinue of coachmen, grooms and stable boys was maintained so that my lady
could drive out in grand style for one-and-a-half hours a day, six days a week.

Conspicuous display reached its most extravagant heights in Hyde Park during the season which was in full swing from Easter to July. Every fine afternoon, a thousand or more carriages would drive along the straight Ladies' Mile, go round the Serpentine and roll back to Hyde Park Corner again. Some of the lady-occupants had just returned from a little light shopping in Regent Street, where by ancient prerogative and custom they were allowed to park their horses and carriages for hours at a time right in the middle of the already congested street. Others were on their way home from a song or a pianoforte recital in some society drawing room, or from a call on an acquaintance who was "at home" that afternoon. Many of them had just gone along for the ride.

Some of the ladies, beautifully attired in the most expensive fashions of the day, drove themselves with a liveried groom sitting on the rumble seat behind, or, occasionally, following on horseback at a distance which was great enough to appear respectful but not so great that he could not afford immediate assistance with horse or carriage in an emergency. The lady drivers carried in their right hand a light whip which they rarely used, whose crop was fitted with a gaily-coloured parasol which was far too minute to be anything but a decorative symbol of their feminity. Other ladies, amply shaded by normal-sized parasols which they held in either hand, were driven by a coachman or a groom, accompanied sometimes by a footman.

All of these servants were dressed in colourful, expensive livery, with gay, vertically striped waistcoats, though the footmen wore horizontal stripes indoors. Their coats were ornamented with silver or gilt livery buttons, embossed with the crest of the family they served, and their shining top hats were usually surmounted by a black leather cockade, indicating that their master held some appointment as an officer or an official from the Crown, the Victorian equivalent of the modern C.D. badge on motor-cars. The stable staff wore highly polished top boots, while the footmen wore white silk stockings which were usually padded out with shapely "falsies" if their calves were thin.

The sunlight glinted on the brightly-polished metal of the leather harness and on the scrupulously clean panels of the carriages, with their painted crest or coat of arms and the family motto, which were in themselves miniature works of art. The horses were all handsome, high-stepping animals. When a pair was used, they were as carefully matched in size as the footmen, who all had to be six feet tall or more.

This daily display of idle opulence had a far more serious purpose than modern readers may think. The ladies smiled, nodded or bowed to other ladies according to their degree of intimacy; or if they happened to see a male acquaintance on the footpath they might stop to have a chat, though between 3 p.m. and 5 p.m. most men were still snoozing in leather armchairs in their clubs, exhausted by luncheon and their earlier exercise on horseback in Rotten Row. Some of the more energetic ladies might have joined the gentlemen in their morning exercise, riding side-saddle, of course, and on alternate sides each day to prevent any undue enlargement of one cheek; but, by the afternoon, they had exchanged their black riding habit for a more colourful afternoon gown and their thoughts had turned from exercise to social advancement, for stocks could rise, and fall, as quickly on Ladies' Mile as they could do in the City, with all the possibilities of a richer social life and a more favourable and profitable match for their daughters.

In Victorian times it was no more permissible for a lower-ranking lady to greet a lady of higher rank with whom she was unacquainted than it was for her to leave her card first at the latter's house: the consequence of such a dreadful solecism would have been a "cut" of which Victorian ladies were superb mistresses, or if the offence were persistent, total ostracism. All the social climbers were alert and vigilant for a nod of recognition from a member of London society which was still in the Seventies and the Eighties, according to one dowager marchioness, "a very definite and a very limited class", restricted to landed proprietors and their wives; permanent Government officials; a select number of London residents; some literary lions, artists and musicians; and a few captains of industry who were just beginning to be recognized.[8] The greatest honour any lady could receive while she was driving in the park was some distant acknowledgement of her existence from Queen Victoria or the Princess of Wales, the future Queen Alexandra. The

A collection of livery buttons showing the crests of some well-known families.

Games	Viscount Milton	Colt Bt.	Acheley	Pardo
Rushton	Ximenes	Beresford	MacDonald	Farquhar

The sociable landau was a favourite carriage for drives in the park.

excitement that the royal bow could produce once led to a highly embarrassing involvement for two young girls, as Lady Clodagh Anson, a daughter of the fifth Marquis of Waterford, recalled. "Two girls we knew once bowed so low to the Princess when they were sitting opposite each other that some wired flower trimming on their large hats got entangled and they could not sit up again; they got the giggles and were quite helpless. Their mother tried to disentangle them . . ."[9] Any gentleman who happened to be driving his own carriage in the park was expected to acknowledge lady friends of acquaintances by raising his hat, though as "Madge" of *Truth* observed, not all men were capable of emulating the chain-smoking Prince of Wales, whom she had once seen smoking one cigar after another for three hours in the Ranelagh Club with only a ten-minute break for tea, by taking "a cigar from his lips and raising his hat with his whip hand, the reins, of course, being in the left".[10] To be a good whip was then a mark of the highest breeding.

Like many other aspects of Victorian life, the carriage world was seasoned with a large measure of deceit. Those magnificent carriage horses held their heads high not through pride, but because they were forced to do so by a savage bit attached to bearing reins: the stamping feet, the foaming mouths and the rattling harnesses were all sure proofs, ignored by gracious ladies, "that their horses are suffering from ceaseless pain".[11] The horses' fine tails were sometimes just as false as the footmen's calves. One "proud peeress", the Countess of Granard, "was not at all amused" when one of her high-stepping horses lost its tail in Regent Street, much to her embarrassment and the amusement of some street urchins, one of whom shouted out with Cockney wit: "Look at the 'orse – 'e's broken 'is tail."[12] The lady smiling graciously behind the plate-glass window of her brougham, which framed the upper half of her splendidly attired torso to perfection, might have been wearing a tattered skirt beneath the frame. Even the brougham she rode in might not have been her own, but had been hired from a jobmaster, who could supply horses, harness, coachman and carriage, even with your own painted crest, for the year, the season, the month, or even the day – at a price. Snobbery moved out of the drawing rooms into the street: the supreme status symbol was to have a well-trained dog "of the plum pudding pattern", with a brass collar round its neck, trotting in unison with the horses behind your carriage.[13]

To support this extravagant display of fashionable folly, there was a great increase in the number of coachbuilders, harness-makers, horse-dealers, livery manufacturers and other associated tradesmen in Victorian times so that by 1872, according to the Post Office London directory, there were no less than 360 blacksmiths in the capital alone, many of whom did much work for the growing carriage trade. This vanished world of carriage folk and coachmen, horse dealers and crooked copers, jobmasters and horse doctors, which did not disappear until the First World War, is one of the least explored but one of the most fascinating public aspects of the great Victorian age, as strange and intriguing in its own way as the parallel, but more private, upstairs-downstairs world within the town houses and country mansions.

(Right above) *A barouche of 1825.*

(Right below) *The Duke of Beaufort, who was one of the country's leading horsemen, insisted that his servants should be of the highest quality.*

BAROUCHE, 1825

HANHART I

THE DRAG

THE PROPERTY OF HIS GRACE THE DUKE OF BEAUFORT, K.G.
PRESIDENT OF THE FOUR-IN-HAND DRIVING CLUB.

2

ARISTOCRATIC SPLENDOUR

In Victorian times no other stables in the whole kingdom could compete in size, spaciousness and splendour with the Royal Mews which had been built in Buckingham Palace Road by John Nash in 1825. The mews contained more servants and officials than horses. The full establishment in the middle of the reign consisted of The Master of the Horse; a principal coachman; twelve coachmen; four footmen; twenty-six grooms; a chief equerry and clerk marshal; four equerries in ordinary; an extra equerry; four pages of honour; a crown equerry and secretary to the Master of the Horse; a first clerk of the stables; an assistant clerk of the stables; an inspector of stables; a veterinary surgeon; a yeoman rider; a lady rider; a serjeant footman; another fifteen footmen; and fifty helpers.[1] Of the hundred or so horses, the most famous were the creams and blacks, of Hanoverian origin like the monarchy, which were used only on great state occasions, when they always appeared with plaited manes, with crimson ribbons for the blacks and purple for the creams. They were never left unattended by day or by night: one of the grooms slept with them at night in the stables.

The coach houses contained the magnificent state coach made for George III in 1762, a pictorial allegory in gold of the history of England with painted panels by the Florentine artist, Giovanni Battista Cipriani; the Irish state coach which was bought by Queen Victoria in 1852; and thirty state and semi-state coaches and carriages. The royal coachmen, all thirteen of them, had four different liveries which had been personally selected by Queen Victoria. The most gorgeous and the most costly was the full state livery worn on the most formal occasions, which

(Left) *The Royal Mews in London is the last living memorial to the splendours of a vanished age.*

The Irish State Coach purchased by Queen Victoria in 1852.

consisted of a scarlet and gold striped frock coat, scarlet knee breeches, pink silk stockings, gold buckled shoes, a wig and a three-cornered hat decorated with pink ostrich feathers; semi-state livery consisting of a scarlet frock coat, white stockings and blue knee breeches; epaulet livery which was similar to the semi-state with boots instead of stockings; and a plain black livery with a white waistcoat for everyday wear. There was a similarly expensive range of different liveries for the grooms, postilions, footmen and pages. Only royal servants had the privilege of wearing the royal cockade, which was oval in shape with a projecting fan, like those worn by the servants of Army officers, only larger.

In the later years of her reign Queen Victoria made very little personal use of her

18

large stud. She had abandoned riding many years before and she had such firm favourites among the hundred horses that the same pair was invariably used to meet her when she arrived by royal train at a London railway station and the same four on her occasional drives in the Park.[2] But in her younger days, before she went into mourning for nearly forty years after the death of Prince Albert in 1861, she had been a keen horsewoman. One of her favourite winter pastimes had been riding in one of her sledges designed by Prince Albert, who had introduced the sport of sleighing from his native Germany. It was no ordinary sleigh ride, but far more like a royal musical on ice. "The Royal Sledge," the *Illustrated London News* reported, "is drawn by two grey horses, across whose back are thrown leopard skins; in the network over the harness are suspended small circular bells, mounted with feathers, besides larger bells which produce three different notes. The body of the Sledge is painted with a dark ground, cross-barred with gold; and the inside is lined with red velvet."[3] On these excursions the queen was accompanied by grooms and outriders in scarlet livery.

Even the richest and most spendthrift aristocrats could not compete with this royal display, though they did as well as they were able. One of the smartest establishments in the early years of the reign was maintained at Gore House, Kensington, by that dark-haired Irish beauty, the Countess of Blessington, and her reputed lover, Count d'Orsay, the son of a French general. The count was a man of many parts being equally renowned as a dandy, a wit, a fencer, a boxer, a shot and a horseman. He was often to be seen in Hyde Park driving his curricle, a swift, stylish, hooded carriage, supported by large C springs, and with a pole and bar instead of shafts so that it could be drawn by a pair of horses. The curricle, which had been popular with dandies since Regency times, was the first carriage bought by Charles Dickens after he had had his first great success with *Pickwick Papers* in 1837. Shortly after that, the curricle was supplanted in the affections of men-about-town by the cabriolet, another two-wheeled vehicle which was not dissimilar in appearance, except that it needed only one horse. D'Orsay was largely responsible for making the cabriolet fashionable by having one built with more elegant lines and larger wheels. He also introduced a new town coach, the Chariot d'Orsay.

For the first twelve years of Victoria's reign, until d'Orsay's extravagance forced the unhappy pair to flee to Paris to escape their debts of £100,000, Gore House was one of the most famous (or infamous) houses in London, not only for the count's trend-setting carriages which came out, but also for the carriages which arrived. Lady Blessington's *salon* became the centre of the literary, artistic and political *avant garde*. Fewer women than men visited her because of her dubious reputation, but one who did so was Mrs. Newton Crosland, the Victorian journalist and novelist, who was overwhelmed by the magnificence of the reception accorded to visitors:

> The great carriage gates were always shut, and it was some one from the stable who answered the loud bell from a small side door. He never knew if his mistress was at home, but took the card that was presented, and in a few minutes, the visitor was admitted to the courtyard. The hall door was flung open by a powdered footman in gorgeous livery of green and gold, and the name passed on to another servitor that looked in every particular his counterpart; both were certainly upwards of six feet in height. The second footman ushered me, on the first visit, into the library.[4]

In contrast to the Blessington-d'Orsay *ménage*, most aristocrats kept their main stud of horses and the majority of their carriages at their ancestral home in the country, bringing up by train to London the servants, carriages and horses that they required for the season. When the Marquis of Bath moved every year to his town house in Berkeley Square, which he exchanged later for one in Grosvenor Square, he used to take with him eleven horses and five members of his stable staff of fourteen, who were all accommodated in the mews behind the big house.[5] Every October or November, the sixth Duke of Richmond and Gordon used to move some of his horses and stable staff from his ancestral home of Goodwood in Sussex up to his town house in London, returning to Goodwood again in July, and in the following month transporting them yet again to his little summer residence of Gordon Castle in Scotland.[6]

The stable block was one of the most conspicuous features of any country mansion of pretensions, second only in size and importance to the main house itself. The stables were usually built around a central quadrangle, a hundred feet by fifty feet or more in area, with an imposing gateway surmounted by a large clock to jog the memory of unpunctual coachmen and by dovecotes, from which white messengers of peace fluttered out during the not infrequent disputes on the ground below. Some stable blocks were of great antiquity, like the one at Wollaton Hall, Nottingham, which was built by Sir Francis Willoughby in the seventeenth century. Its magnificence made a great impression on the writer of a Victorian guide book published in 1856:

> The central portion of the façade contains a grand arched gateway below, surmounted by a circular clock face above it; it is flanked by ornamental pillars, and

The curricle, a favourite carriage amongst men-about-town.

pilasters, and terminates in a tympanium, bearing an exceedingly florid, large and beautiful sculpture of the royal arms, which is greatly coveted and admired. The internal capacity and arrangements of the stables, extending to thirty-five single stalls, with accommodation for sixty horses if required, by no means belie the expectations created by this imposing exterior. The stud stands as a nobleman's horses should, in a beautifully kept, almost palatial, set of six feet stalls, with clean-looking, buff-coloured divisions, striped with broad black bars . . . A large solid oak block of now perfectly black, indeed, pure, ebony, adopted thirty-five years ago by the late Lord Middleton for a mounting block lies in the front range of stables.[7]

Wherever possible, stables were built on a gravel slope to assist in drainage, and facing south or south-west, as horses, like human beings, eat less if they are warm and comfortable. The stables had to be well-ventilated, though not draughty, if the horses were not to be subject to perpetual bouts of flu; and they had to be large enough to accommodate the horses of visitors. The largest stables were divided into separate sections for carriage horses, riding horses, hunters, and visitors' horses.

The stable block also contained one or two coach houses which could hold up to seven or eight carriages. The coach houses were sometimes equipped with wheel tracks to prevent damage to the valuable carriages when they were wheeled in and out. There was also a harness room, which often served as the coachman's office, with its hanging sets of single, pair, tandem and team harnesses; saddles; and a glass case full of highly-polished steel bits which shone like silver. In the largest stables, there was also a grooming shed, a shoeing shed and a smithy. The grooms and stable lads usually lived above the hay and corn lofts in a mess room, crudely furnished with a few benches and a table, a cupboard and a range, and which reeked of ammonia from the stalls below, though as one Victorian architect complacently remarked, servants did not seem to mind the smell.[8] Their sleep was often disturbed by the stamping and kicking of the horses at night. In larger establishments the head coachman lived in a cottage or a lodge: his wife had the extra, unpaid duty of opening the gates to carriages. Some coachmen had their meals in the servants' hall in the big house, but most of them ate at home and received board wages in lieu of free food.

In Victorian times, many ancient stable blocks were modernized to provide greater comfort for the horses, but far less frequently for the stable staff. The old stone or cobbled surface of the central courtyard was ripped out and replaced by a less slippery pavement; iron mangers, troughs and hay racks were substituted for the old wooden ones; and some stalls were converted into twelve by fourteen feet loose boxes to give the horses more leg room. Slow combustion stoves were installed in coach houses to protect the carriages from damp; and Turkish baths were added to some stables to comfort horses suffering from exhaustion or influenza, a refinement that the stable staff – and the mass of the working classes – might have appreciated even more as, at that time, virtually none of them had the use of any bath at all – Turkish or English.

Americans could not fail to contrast the living conditions that English aristocrats provided for their horses and their servants or tenants. After Benjamin Moran, an American diplomat, had visited Wentworth Hall, Rotherham, Yorkshire, one of the ancestral homes of Earl Fitzwilliam, he wrote: "The stalls for the horses were better built and cleaner than many of the cottages on the estate, and the horses better cared for than the peasantry. The structure is of stone, built in the form of a hollow square, with a court-yard in which a gurgling fountain plays constantly. The stalls for the animals are ceiled and plastered, which is more than can be said for one-half the English cottages."[9]

Aristocrats were just as fastidious about their horses as their stables. Appearance was far more important than speed or stamina. "The carriage-horse of the present day is essentially a horse more for pleasure than for use," wrote Samuel Sidney in 1881.[10] They all had to be handsome, high-stepping animals and perfectly matched when a pair was used; but their colour was far more a matter of personal preference which sometimes had an ulterior significance. In Regency times, Viscount Petersham, who designed the heavy overcoat which bears his name, drove around in a brown curricle, drawn by brown horses, and with a groom in brown livery as a public proclamation of his devotion to a Mrs. Brown, just as some purchased motor-car registration plates of today indicate the initials of a mistress. One grey-haired lady, who always dressed in grey, insisted on having horses of the same colour, so that any horse hairs blown back on her while she was out in her carriage should not mar her harmonious appearance. Viscount Palmerston and his wife both favoured grey horses. He had his own grey horse for riding in Hyde Park, which was "the despair" of his wife, with four grey carriage horses of her own, as she "feared lest people should think that her husband rode one of them".[11] Chestnut horses were never used for carriage work in the Royal Mews, but Lord Michelham, who presented the nation with the sculptured chariot and ponies which adorn the top of the arch at Hyde Park Corner, would have nothing else. Horace Smith, the royal riding master who taught the present queen to ride, recalls how in his earlier days as a horse dealer, he used to take horses to this eccentric peer's home in Prince's Gate for his inspection. Lord Michelham was an excellent judge of horseflesh; but he needed the stimulus of music to make up his mind. If he took a fancy to a horse he would invite Smith to come inside the house to share in the musical interlude between thought and decision. "On either side of the main entrance hall," Smith recalls, "was an imposing-looking door which led into a huge reception room. We would enter the right-hand door and my host would turn to his butler and say 'Start the brass band'. Then from the depths of some hidden alcove in the wall would come the strains of martial music, which continued until the order came to 'Stop the Music'. We would then turn on our heels and move smartly into the opposite room. 'Start the strings' ordered the master, and immediately from a similarly concealed alcove came a programme of classical music, played by an invisible orchestra. In the meantime, my unconventional host strutted, danced and cavorted around the room in time to the music. He was an odd volume, right enough, but a likeable man and a great judge of a horse."[12]

(Overleaf) *This magnificent watercolour drawing of Belgrave Square by Eugene Lami dated 1880 shows how the two worlds lived.*

23

The cabriolet replaced the curricle as a fashionable vehicle for society men in the early years of Queen Victoria's reign.

The best carriage horses were brought to London when they were about four years old and were given an eight-month course in deportment by horse dealers. These dealers, who invested thousands of pounds in horses and their own judgment, showed no mercy to recalcitrant pupils: those who refused to learn the necessary skills were sent off to haul a heavy omnibus for a year as a punishment, before they were brought back to try again.[13] Horse breakers taught the horse how to stand well; to turn gracefully; to stop stylishly; to carry its head well (with or without the use of bearing reins); and to acquire the mandatory high-stepping action, even though, as the Earl of Onslow pointed out, "the concussion which his feet suffer every time he brings them down on the road cannot fail to prove detrimental to their soundness".[14] In spite of this eminent horseman's warning, expensive horses continued to be sacrificed to fashion in that age of conspicuous display.

One of the cruellest whims of fashion was the docking of horses' tails, which had been all the mode in Regency times, and which was revived again in the 1870s.

Docking, which caused great controversy at the time, involved the amputation of several vertebrae in the tail and the searing of the bleeding stump with a hot iron. Sometimes the shortened tail was also nicked to make it stand upright. The remaining vertebrae were partially cut through on the underside to sever the tendon which pulls the tail down. The tail was initially kept in an upright position by tying it to a weight suspended from an overhead pulley.[15]

Some fashion-conscious aristocrats tried to justify docking on the ground that it prevented the horse from switching its tail over the reins or splashing dirt in the driver's face; but many people, including the sixth Duke of Portland and Queen Alexandra were strongly opposed to this barbaric practice, while the Royal Society for the Prevention of Cruelty to Animals conducted a long campaign against this "crime" which deprived the horse of its natural fly-swat. Queen Alexandra was once involved in an embarrassing situation when a group of Canadian ladies presented her with two native-born horses, whose tails had been docked without authority by an ignorant veterinary surgeon before shipment. If she refused to accept the horses, she would have offended the Canadian ladies; but if she kept them, she would have offended her own principles. The problem was solved by sending the two horses back to Canada again so that they could be replaced by the vet – at his own expense.[16]

The most popular breeds of horses for carriage work were Cleveland Bays, Yorkshire coach horses and Hackneys, though with the great increase in demand for harness horses as the reign progressed, the world was searched for substitutes, which were imported from many different countries, including Germany, Hungary and the United States. Most of the highest-priced harness horses were docile geldings; stallions were scarcely ever used, though they were commonly employed in many Continental countries. In the 1890s, a reasonable carriage horse could cost £100 to £150; but a perfectly matched pair of the finest quality could cost as much as £500 or even £1,000.

Wealthy aristocrats were just as extravagant in their purchase of carriages. The most prized possession in their coach house was the state or town coach, which seated four people face to face, or the lighter dress chariot, which seated only two, and usually had a miniature painted crest on the door panels instead of the coach's more flamboyant coat of arms. At Wollaton Hall in 1856, as in other great country houses, "the old yellow family coach" still stood in state "with full heraldic bearings and crest of the family, motto and all, *Verité sans Peur* (Truth void of fear), emblazoned on its panels".[17] In troubled times, these ancient public symbols of wealth and privilege could attract the angry resentment of radicals, though the aristocratic smile could then still sometimes have a disarming effect. Countess Brownlow remembered how she was driving along Piccadilly during the Reform riots of 1830, when the country was on the verge of civil war, and a "mean-looking shabby little man on a wretched horse trotted to the side of my carriage, examined the arms on the panels, the coronet on the top, the footmen behind, and then with a most disagreeable expression of countenance stared at me. I did not quite like it, but I smiled at him as if I did," and he cantered off.[18] Other ladies were not so fortunate, or, perhaps, they did not have the same gracious smile. Lady Clodagh Anson recalls the later "bread riots in London, and hearing awful stories of ladies in victorias being attacked, the coachmen being hauled off their boxes and all their clothes torn off, which shocked us very deeply."[19]

These coaches continued to be used throughout the Victorian age on ceremonial and social occasions. Less than a century ago, every night during the season, they would roll and rumble out of the mews at the back of fashionable streets and squares in London to take the highest-born aristocrats – and some bishops – to dinner parties, the opera and receptions. If the family was going to the theatre, they would dine at 6.30 p.m. and order their carriages for eight so that they would reach the theatre in good time for the performance which started just before nine o'clock and sometimes continued to 12.30 or 1 in the morning. "The carriages," according to one contemporary observer, "were drawn by satin-skinned chestnuts or superb greys, with silver-plated harness; the carriages, in the midst of whose sumptuous hammercloths, blazing with armorial bearings, sit coachmen with spun-glass wigs, and pink silk stockings, and to whose back straps hang gigantic flunkeys in plush and powder."[20] The crush of high-hung coaches and aristocratic carriages was sometimes so great at evening receptions that, to keep the traffic moving, aristocrats with names of ancient lineage were forced to give way to those with far more plebian surnames. One American visitor was astonished by the democratic equality at the end of a reception given by Lady Rosebery at the Foreign Office in 1886. "A crowd of anxious persons in retreat," wrote Oliver Wendell Holmes, "is hanging about the windy door, and the breezy stairway, and the airy hall. A stentorian voice . . . exclaims – 'Lady Vere de Vere's carriage stops the way!'

"If my Lady Vere de Vere is not on hand, and that pretty quickly, off goes her carriage, and the stern voice bawls again – 'Mrs. Smith's carriage stops the way!'"[21]

The coaches were also used on court days, such as the state opening of parliament. Coachmen, who were often more conservative and conscious of status than

A brougham preserved in the Glasgow Museum of Transport.

their masters (if not their mistresses), took a great delight in dressing up in their plush knee breeches, silk stockings and ornate coats and in decorating their horses with all the conventional appendages for these occasions. The English coachman of the American minister's wife in London was profoundly shocked when he discovered that, in her ignorant American way, she had forgotten to order "the pads, the fronts, and the handpieces" for her glass-fronted coach for the state opening of parliament. He told her in a patronizing way: "Why, ma'am, we always has pads under the saddle on Court days, trimmed round with the colours of the livery, and we has fronts made of ribbins for the horses' heads, and we has white hand-pieces for the reins."[22]

In addition to his state or town coach, the wealthy aristocrat would have had six or seven other carriages in his coach houses, selected according to the size of his fortune and family, and his personal needs and preferences. Some aristocrats remained obstinately attached to their old-style carriages long after the fashion for them had passed. A few curricles were still in use in the Seventies and Eighties. The cabriolet remained a favourite vehicle among a few rich Guards officers, stockbrokers, and dandies of the past, who liked to maintain the fashion of their youth if they were still active enough to do so, as the cabriolet, with its high curved body and its step attached to one of the shafts, was not the easiest carriage to get into, so that the Duke of Cambridge, who had too great a partiality to public dinners, had to be practically manhandled into his by two footmen. But, by the Seventies, most of the old-style carriages and coaches, such as curricles, cabriolets, travelling coaches, chariots and many others had disappeared and others, such as tilburies, dennets, britzskas and vis-à-vis had become almost as remote to the new generation as they certainly are to the present one. Nevertheless, there was still a bewildering choice of carriages. By the Eighties, there were no less than thirty-three main types, each with innumerable variations and minor modifications, to choose from.

One of the most popular Victorian carriages was the coachman-driven brougham, a small closed vehicle of French origin, seating two people, which Lord Brougham had redesigned in 1838 as "a refined and glorified street cab that would make a convenient carriage for a gentleman".[23] A brougham cost about £150, though a miniature brougham, which was much favoured by young Guards officers, could be bought for £20 or £30 less. There was also a coupé, or double, brougham, drawn by a pair of horses, and seating four, which was a popular choice among aristocrats with a large brood of daughters.

The lady of the house needed her own carriage for shopping, visiting and driving

The dog cart was a useful little carriage for going to the shoot, or meeting guests at the railway station.

in the park. For this purpose, the victoria was eminently suitable, particularly as it had been named after the queen and therefore had a great snob appeal. The victoria was a low-built vehicle with an elegantly-curved body and had no doors to impede ladies in their voluminous dresses from getting in and out. There were mudguards to prevent dirt from being thrown up on to their faces, and a small leather hood to protect them from showers but not from storms, so that they sometimes returned from their excursions in the park, shivering and drenched to the skin. On sunny days, however, they could loll back in their padded seats, holding their coloured parasol aloft, and displaying to an admiring world their toilet from the crown of their head to the sole of their foot. "What the brougham is for the face of beauty," wrote Sidney, "the victoria is for the robes – a frame for one, a pedestal for the other."[24] Although the carriage itself cost only £100 or so, it needed a horse, or a pair, of the most expensive kind and a high-class coachman and a footman in livery on the box if it was to draw the eyes of the crowd, which was what driving was then all about. Some ladies preferred to do their own driving in a

31

park phaeton, which was not unlike the victoria in appearance except that it had no coachman's box. (The prototype had been built for the gross and gouty George IV who found it difficult in old age to get in and out of anything but a low-built carriage.)

Larger vehicles were also used for driving in the park, including the barouche which was the equivalent among open carriages of the town coach among the closed, as it needed a pair of the largest and most expensive horses. The barouche could be used only in fine weather since it had only a small folding hood which protected only two of the four passengers when it rained. Increasingly, the barouche was replaced by the sociable landau, which had leather hoods at the back and at the front so that it could be used in fair weather and in foul. The sociable landau was expensive, costing about £200, but it was equally suitable for use in the town and in the country.

Other carriages were designed more for use than for display. One of the most popular was the four-wheeled waggonette which had been introduced by Prince Albert in the middle of the 1840s. It could seat up to six people, three on each side facing each other, and had ample locker space for the ice, wine and other delicacies which were essential ingredients of those immensely popular Victorian picnics, or for guns and rods for a more serious day's work. The waggonette was not dissimilar in appearance to the dog cart which must not be confused with the common cart drawn by a dog, whose use was prohibited in London in 1839 and in the rest of the country by 1855. The aristocratic dog cart was originally designed to carry the dogs in the ventilated boot out for a day's sport in the countryside. Later, it became an all-purpose vehicle used by the master or the groom to meet house guests at the railway station, or by the lady to visit the nearest town. There were also larger vehicles such as private omnibuses and char-a-bancs and many more.

To look after all their carriages and horses, the richest aristocrats employed up to thirty men in their stables, though a smaller number was more common. The Duke of Westminster, one of the richest men in England with an income of £250,000 a year from his London estate alone, kept only three coachmen and twelve grooms at Eaton Hall in Cheshire in the later years of the century, though

(Right above) *A waggonette built by Hamshaw of Leicester in the second half of the nineteenth century.*

(Right below) *A phaeton, which was a popular carriage for ladies driving in the park.*

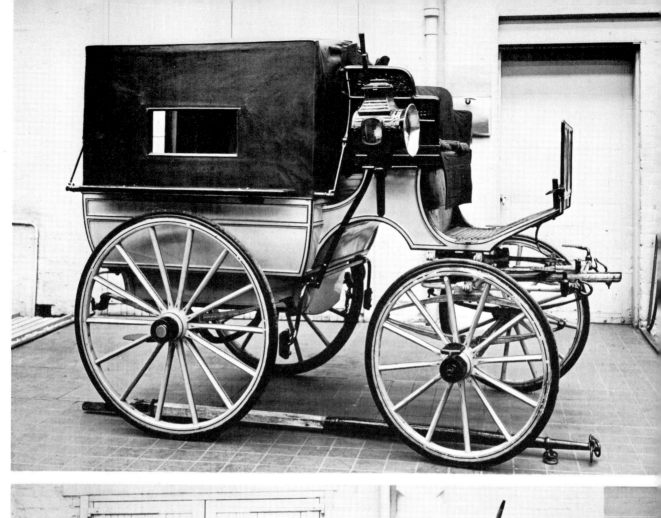

he also had a Shire horse stud groom with six grooms under him and a racing stud manager with a head groom and thirty men and boys.[25] At about the same time, the Marquis of Bath employed fourteen men in his stables at Longleat, Wiltshire, including a coachman and a second coachman, a carriage groom and a "steel boy", whose only task was to polish the bits and the metal parts of the harness. There was also a fully-equipped blacksmith's shop, which was visited once a fortnight by the local blacksmith from Horningsham.[26] A little later on, in the transitional period when both carriages and motor cars were used, the sixth Duke of Portland maintained a more than adequate stable and garage at Welbeck Abbey. In the former he employed a head coachman, a second coachman, ten grooms and twenty helpers; and in the latter, a head chauffeur, fifteen chauffeurs, fifteen footmen and two car washers. He also had a racing stable with a stud groom and fifteen assistants.[27]

Although the stable staff and the head coachman in particular were entrusted with the care of horses and carriages worth thousands of pounds, their wages scarcely corresponded with their responsibilities, as aristocrats had a tendency to combine "ostentation with economy" not only with their servants but also sometimes with their guests. Mary Paley Marshall, a rector's daughter, remembered how she used to visit the local big house in the 1860s, whose owners "drove about in a carriage and pair with a coachman and footman in crimson plush smalls and white stockings. But once when I went there to tea with a boy friend a solitary strawberry was divided between us 'because it was so big', and the drawing room had its furniture swathed in brown holland and was only used on grand occasions."[28]   In the Eighties, head coachmen in some aristocratic establishments received only about £1 a week. At Goodwood House in 1888, the Duke of Richmond and Gordon was paying his head coachman £52 10s. a year, less than his house steward, his groom of the chambers (a sort of super butler) and his valet.[29] In a few bigger establishments some head coachmen received about 50% more. The under coachman at Goodwood was paid £35 a year and footmen, who were graded in rank from first to third, got £26 to £34 a year. The wages of grooms varied considerably, some of them receiving almost as much as the second coach-

(Left above) *This family coach was built by Rawlins of London in 1817.*

(Left below) *Carriages designed for men-about-town also had graceful lines and a diminutive seat for the groom at the rear.*

One of the black state horses – Zulu – in 1890 harness for a big occasion.

man and others receiving only about £20 a year. Stable lads earned even less. In addition, they were all provided with free accommodation and free food or board wages in lieu.

The coachmen, grooms and footmen were also provided with free liveries, usually two full sets a year. These expensive, fancy dress costumes came in three varieties: full state livery with wigs, knee breeches, stockings and tricorne hats for use with the town coach or the chariot; a less elaborate costume for everyday wear consisting of frock coat, great coat, striped waistcoats, top hat, and breeches and top boots for the stable staff; and a working dress of coat, cord breeches and overalls. Liveries were usually provided in April so that they could bedazzle the rest of the world during the height of the season. Reverence for rank and status was no less strong among outdoor staff than it was inside the big house, where upper servants ate their pudding separately from the lower servants and valets and ladies' maids adopted their master's and mistress's aristocratic names in place of their own surnames. In the stables, rank was reflected in the livery: the coachman's frock coat had flaps at the sides while the groom's had none. Their livery was ornamented with special buttons embossed with the family crest and made of silver or gilt according to whether the family's coat of arms was described as *argent* or *or*.[30]

34

The cost of maintaining these extravagant establishments of servants and stables was enormous. Aristocrats seem to have spent on average between one-sixth and one-fifth of their income on their stables. In 1839, the Earl of Ashburnham's horses and carriages took almost one-fifth of his annual household expenditure of £3,000.[31] There were also taxes on male servants, carriages, horses for riding, and the use of armorial bearings on carriages, which, in his case, amounted to over £100 a year.[32] In addition, there was the initial cost of the horses and carriages which increased by about two-and-a-half times between 1832 and 1876.

By the Seventies the great agricultural depression was just beginning to make savage cuts in the incomes of aristocrats who depended too heavily on rents from farm land. There was consternation in many big house and anxious daytime meetings and sleepless nights over how they could ever make ends meet. Lord Ashburnham had contingency plans drawn up to counter the great crisis in his financial affairs. He decided that he would have to give up his horses and take to Shank's mare instead by dismissing "the first and second footmen, coachman, stable helper, groom, hall boy and a few others", which would in all have saved him over £300 a year. He also planned to open a corner shop in the nearby town of St. Leonards to sell fruit, vegetables and cut flowers from his estate at Ashburnham Place, Sussex.[33]

Costs continued to mount in an alarming fashion. In 1889, it was estimated that it cost £782 a year to keep the minimum establishment for any man with pretensions to fashion, consisting of two coachmen, a helper, and six horses, who were in the London mews for four months and in the country stables for the rest of the year.[34] At that period, the Duke of Richmond and Gordon was spending almost £1,500 a year in stable expenses, which included the cost of forage and repairs, board wages, veterinary surgeon's fees, the wages of helpers, and out-of-pocket expenses, but not the wages or liveries of higher stable staff.[35]

Before the end of the century many of the richest aristocrats had decided that it was cheaper to hire carriage horses from one of the great London jobmasters for the season. Even royalty was not unaffected by the rise in costs. In 1873, Col. G. A. Maude, Secretary to the Master of the Horse, told one official inquiry that "there are smaller carriages than there used to be, such as broughams and clarences", in the Royal Mews and that smaller horses would also have been used "if it were not for the look of the thing".[36] But in the end, even Queen Victoria had to use the services of a jobmaster on some special occasions.

3

LIFE IN MEWS AND STABLES

To support all this pomp and pageantry in the park, there was a very different kind of overcrowded, fly-infested world concealed at the back of gracious squares and sandwiched between the wide streets in such fashionable districts as Mayfair, Westminster and Kensington. Until the Eighties, mews were usually provided whenever a terrace of society houses was built. For example, 670 houses were built between Princes Gate Mews and the top of Queen's Gate in South Kensington between 1855 and the early 1880s, and 480 coach houses and stables were constructed at the same time.[1] In the most fashionable streets and squares, all the houses had their own coach houses and stables in adjacent mews on a one-to-one basis.

Although some property speculators, who were just as common in Victorian times as they are today, tried to charge excessive rents for London stables at a rate of £45 a horse, a mews could usually be rented for a third or a half of that cost. In 1867, the Mitfords of Tillington, Sussex, let a London mews consisting of a coach house and three stables with a loft above, for £35 a year.[2] To save expensive space, two-storey mews were built increasingly in Victorian times, with the coach house on the ground floor and the stables, approached by a ramp, on the floor above with a gallery, protected by iron railings, where the horses could be groomed. One of the first two-storey mews was built by Mr. Henry Hope behind his mansion opposite Green Park with disastrous results for himself and his neighbours. He drained the stables into the public sewers, which was no more pleasant for nearby residents than it was successful for him, as, at that time, the sewers gave off even more noxious fumes than a normal clean-littered stable, with the result that he lost most of his expensive stud.[3]

Some of the London mews were impressively grand, like one in Sackville Street, off Piccadilly, with its handsome entrance gates, its two coach houses, its loose

36

boxes and its separate stalls for horses on night duty.[4] Mews of that size could accommodate two riding horses; a pair of carriage horses for the lady's exclusive use; two "slaves" or screws for night work; and three leaders, which could be used for a victoria or phaeton, and three wheelers, which were more suitable for a brougham or landau, and which, together, could be used as a team, with the leaders in front, to haul a large state or town coach.[5] Most mews, however, particularly those of permanent residents of the professional classes, were far less commodious. These mews, which can still be seen in many parts of central London to this day, could usually hold only two carriages, a brougham for the master and a victoria or a landau for the mistress, which had to be parked behind each other in the small coach house with all the consequent inconvenience in wheeling them in and out, and three or four horses in constricted and often ill-ventilated stables. The coachman and his family lived in a set of small rooms on the first floor approached by a steep, narrow, dark staircase. The mews were overshadowed by the big houses, which turned their ugly backs on the miniature world on which they depended but which they did not wish to know.

Although these coach houses and stables have now been converted into garages, workshops, offices, and even sitting rooms, the mews still possess a very definite character of their own, an atmosphere which was even more pungent in Victorian times when they introduced into the heart of fashionable London the sounds and smells of the countryside and a collection of characters who always seem to congregate round horses like flies: commission agents, touts, copers, dealers, corn chandlers, bookmakers, strappers and casual labourers. "The mews of London," wrote Henry Mayhew, that expert on the underside of Victorian life, in 1861, "constitute a world of their own. They are tenanted by one class – coachmen and grooms, with their wives and families – men who are devoted to one pursuit, the care of horses and carriages; who live and associate one among another; whose talk is of horses (with something about masters and mistresses) as if to ride or to drive were the great ends of human existence and who thus live as much together as the Jews in their compulsory quarters in Rome."[6] This self-involved world did not open its gates easily to strangers; but it provided a refuge for many a coachman or a groom who was down on his luck, for it was united not only by work, gossip and interests, but also often by blood. Eighty-seven-year-old Mr. Robert Barley, one of the few surviving former jobmasters, recalls that many of the coachmen in the capital's mews were London-born men and that their sons often obtained jobs as footmen in the big house and received their first instructions in the art of driving when they went out with their fathers on the box.[7] In Victorian times the larger

Even the richest aristocrats could not afford to have London stables as spacious as the Royal Mews.

mews saved many an unfortunate coachman or groom from the indignities of the workhouse at the end of his life. Mayhew described how he talked to one old, consumptive man who lived in a long, low room with his wife and son above some stables in Tottenham Mews. He had once worked as a groom for Viscount Combermere, but had left his employment some years before and eked out a living by polishing harness for a few pence. His room was barely furnished with two "turn-up" beds and a few prized mementoes of his sad life: a large lithograph of a horse; a Hogarth etching in a black frame; a stuffed bird in a wooden cage; and a few china ornaments. His wife was equally old and helpless and his thirty-seven-year-old son, who was lame, purblind and of subnormal intelligence, made a few pence a week by working as a crossing sweeper.[8]

In the height of the season, the mews were restless with activity for almost twenty-four hours a day. Ernest Shephard, the illustrator of A. A. Milne's *Winnie-the-Pooh*, recalls how as a young boy in the Eighties, he used to visit the mews near his home in St. John's Wood, which was "a most interesting place with plenty going on – horses being groomed or harnessed, carriages washed or polished, the grooms hissing and whistling at their work. Strings of washing hung from the upper windows, whence the womenfolk leaned out and chatted to the men below."[9] There was no division between public and private life: activity spilled out of the coach house and the stables into the street, and the smells of the stables were carried up to the rooms above, though the occupants were far less conscious of them than we might be today, as in those days a miasma of manure hung like a mist over the capital, and coachmen and grooms liked the smell of a clean, well-tended stable and were offended only if their noses detected negligence.

Work started in the mews (as it did in country stables) at 5 a.m. in the summer and 6 a.m. in the winter so that the head coachman, after having a late breakfast at 10 a.m., could report at the big house to receive the orders of the day, confident in the knowledge that he could turn out well-groomed horses and immaculate carriages, without a speck of dirt inside or outside, within twenty minutes of his master's or mistress's command. Before he had his breakfast the stables had to be cleaned, the horses had to be groomed and fed, and the carriages and harnesses had to be polished. The coachman usually groomed the carriage horses, while the groom looked after the riding horses. Each horse was thoroughly cleaned from the tip of its ears to the soles of its feet to free its skin of all accumulated scurf, dirt and sweat. The ears were gently massaged for a few minutes until they were warm and then wiped out with a damp sponge; the hooves were washed and the dirt picked out before they were anointed in Victorian times with a mixture of oil and lamp black in the mistaken belief that it would increase the growth of the horn. The whole process took about one-and-a-half hours and at the end of it the master expected the coat to be so clean that it would not "soil a cambric handkerchief".[10]

The carriages were thoroughly cleaned, the body with a soft sponge or a cloth mop, the wheels with a spoke brush, and the leather braces with an oily rag. Servants were also expected to check each carriage for safety, though they were often negligent in this respect, which sometimes had disastrous consequences for their employers. "I myself," complained Sir George Stephen ruefully, "received a concussion of the brain from the neglect of my servant in passing over a broken shaft in my stanhope, that he daily cleaned."[11] The harness also had to be polished and inspected. Sir George, who, understandably, had become one of the keenest advocates of safety precautions, recommended that buckles should be undone and checked at regular intervals as "every coachman knows that nine times out of ten the trace breaks at the tongue of the buckle".[12]

Although we may grumble when our motor-car fails to start, we could gain some consolation from the experiences of our Victorian ancestors. In those days there was no possibility of stepping into a vehicle and going out for a drive straight away. The smartest carriages were not ready for use until eleven in the morning and even when they were ordered, it took at least another twenty minutes for the carriage to be wheeled out and the horses harnessed, before it could be driven round from the mews to the front door of the big house. These time-consuming processes all had to be repeated whenever a horse or a carriage was used, not only for the sake of appearance but also for the protection of the large financial investment. It was little wonder that if a carriage was to be used only three times a day it was necessary to employ two coachmen and two grooms.[13]   It was the head coachman's responsibility to see that everything in the mews was kept in a first-rate condition. Employers preferred their head coachmen to be between thirty and forty years of age. Before thirty they were often too perfunctory and lacking in authority; after forty they were sometimes too dim-sighted, drunk or lazy to be of much use. Having come up from the ranks themselves, head coachmen retained a firm belief in the value of "spit and polish", authority, and deference to rank. Most high-class coachmen modelled their behaviour on the pattern established in the Royal Mews where, in Victorian times, "an almost military discipline is maintained".[14] Words were never wasted on stable boys when a length of harness was always at hand. Grooms could be, and were, dismissed on the spot for any negligence.

London coachmen competed with each other in turning out the most magnificent equipages, which was one of the reasons that the fashion for bearing reins lasted so long. They all had their patent remedies and panaceas for horse ailments, even though these more often killed than cured: a titled lady's coachman once gave two of her valuable horses his patent remedy for influenza, which successfully killed both of them off within forty-eight hours. Head coachmen, or their wives, spent many hours crouched over some cauldron in the stables or the mews, cooking up their special brews. One recipe for liquid blacking used in cleaning harness ran:

> Take 2 oz. of mutton suet, melted; 6 oz. of purified beeswax, melted; ¼ lb. of lamp black; 1 gill of turpentine; 2 oz. of Prussian blue, powdered; 1 oz. of indigo blue, ground; 6 oz. of sugar candy, melted in a little water; and 2 oz. of soft soap. Mix, and simmer over the fire 15 minutes, then add a gill of turpentine.[15]

Most of these arcane concoctions were unnecessary: the Prince of Wales's coach-

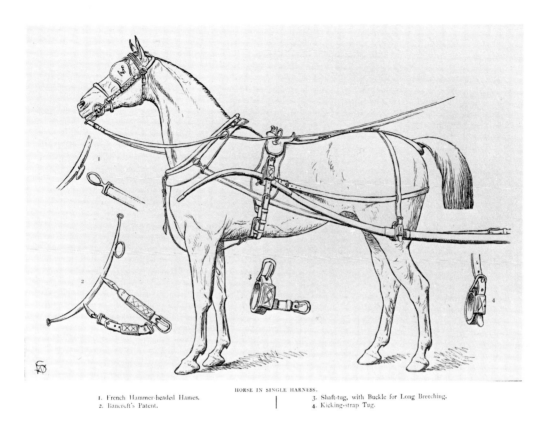

1. French Hammer-headed Hames.
2. Bancroft's Patent.

HORSE IN SINGLE HARNESS.

3. Shaft-tug, with Buckle for Long Breeching.
4. Kicking-strap Tug.

An illustration from Cassell's Book of the Horse.

man had the smartest harness in town by using no more special a preparation than Everett's Liquid Blacking, which was commonly used then for cleaning boots and shoes.[16]

The head coachman drove the main carriage in the daytime. He needed to be a man of imposing presence for "on the sobriety, steady conduct, and respectable appearance of this important servant, depend the exterior appearance of the family with which he resides".[17] Above all, he needed to be a skilful driver. It was, indeed, no easy task then to drive a carriage through the crowded city streets, swiftly, surely, and without excessive use of the whip, coming to a halt so smoothly at a succession of houses or shops that the passengers were not flung to the floor.

Masters like the Duke of Beaufort, who had spent (or misspent) much of their youth on the box of a stagecoach learning to drive, demanded the highest standards from their coachman. Not only would they have refused to pardon such mishaps, in the duke's own words, "as flicking a gentleman under the ear or sending the dirty end of the whip round someone's face", but they would also have been equally critical of "that dreadful sight, which is to be seen a hundred and more times every day in the streets of London, of gentlemen and their coachmen (gardeners, I ought to say) driving one or a pair with their hands close up to their noses, and a rein in each hand".[18] His coachmen were expected to drive correctly and in the only safe way, with the reins in their left hand, the whip in the right, both hands held low and their elbows tucked into their sides. Good driving depended on delicacy of touch, as masters were always willing to demonstrate with brusque Victorian rudeness to their servants. One gentleman tied a rope to a pole and gave the other end to his groom.

"Now pull," said he and the groom pulled.

"Do you feel it pulling?" said the gentleman.

"Yes," replied the groom.

"Now slacken it off; does it pull now?"

"No," answered the groom.

"Now, you fool," said the gentleman, "that post is like your horses; if you don't pull at them, they won't pull at you!"[19]

Masters who might relapse into gloomy and prolonged silence when any general topic was being discussed over port or claret, or when their wives were pestering them with some fine detail of household business, could become loud-mouthed martinets in their own mews and stables. "Gentlemen," wrote Sir George Stephen, "are always more fidgety and precise on matters that relate to their pleasures, than on other points of domestic economy. If the guns are not in order, or the kennel, or the billiard room, and, above all, the stable, more dissatisfaction is expressed than if the dinner is spoilt, or the wardrobe deranged."[20] Squire Waterton, of Walton Hall, Worcestershire, had an inflexible rule that his horses should not be tethered at night, and was so infuriated when he found a horse tied up that he cut the halter into little pieces. The next morning his bailiff started to apologize by saying: "Please, sir, I thowt ..."

"You *thowt*. YOU thowt!" shouted the enraged squire. "Nobody thinks here but me."[21]

Mistresses were no less domineering than their husbands, and sometimes far more ignorant and inconsiderate. Some ladies made a habit of overloading their carriage with too many large parcels and fat friends, which brought the master's wrath down on the unfortunate coachman for letting the horses get out of condition. If the horse moved in its collar when the mistress stepped gracefully into the

42

High-class coachmen were expected to display the correct method of driving, especially when they were on the way to Hurlingham.

carriage, or if she ever had to repeat her instructions, she would invariably suspect, sometimes correctly, that the coachman had been at the bottle again. It was virtually impossible for a coachman who had been dismissed for drunkenness, real or suspected, to get a job in a society household again.

Society people often had a much greater concern for their horses than their stable staff. Although the under coachman, who did most of the night driving, was expected to wait around for hours in rain, fog, sleet or snow, while the master and the mistress were enjoying themselves in some warm dining room or theatre, the best horses were never taken out at night, but only inferior ones, "slaves" or screws, as "no one who values a good horse would dream of allowing him to stand exposed to chilly blasts at the opera, the theatre, or his club".[22] In 1852, Henry White was working as a coachman for three God-fearing ladies who went out to late parties "three nights out of the six". One bitterly cold night, he went to fetch them from a party and sent word into the house that he had arrived. They came out gaily an hour later, when he remarked that he was "almost frozen". Graciously, they allowed him to drive them home; but he was dismissed for impudence the next morning.[23]

Grooms did some riding and driving in addition to their stable duties. They were expected to accompany the master when he went out driving as the coachman considered it beneath his dignity to do so. They often accompanied their master when he went out riding, following on horseback at a respectful distance. They also travelled with him in a dog cart to the meet of hounds, with two horses in tandem, one in front of the other, so that the master's hunter in front could be unharnessed at the meet and the groom could drive the carriage home. Grooms (and stable lads) were usually the first people to be blamed if anything went wrong in the stables. Some of them were ignorant and unskilled men, who made a habit of cutting off the haw, or third eyelid, of the horse whenever it became inflamed and protruded, with the result that the horse often became totally or partially blind, as the haw is used to clean the eye of dust and insects.[24] Some masters, however, were even more ignorant than their grooms. An Army officer once complained to Mr. Field of Oxford Street, one of the best-known and most quick-witted Victorian vets, that he had been forced to dismiss his groom because he had thrown a horse down. Mr. Field replied: "Have the kindness to send him to me . . . He will be very valuable, as I often want a horse thrown down, and have to employ five or six men to do it!"[25]

Footmen were not members of the stable hierarchy, but ornamental appendages. They worked in the house during the morning, cleaning the gold and silver plate, scrubbing their mistress's small change to prevent her from being infected by tradesmen's germs, and waiting at the luncheon table. For the rest of the day, and sometimes many hours of the night, too, they could be out with the carriages. These handsome fellows, some of whom were six feet six inches tall, had trained themselves to act in unison. When they arrived at the house of call, they would step down smartly from the carriage together, march across the pavement like soldiers on parade, knock thunderously at the double knocker in unison, and then march back to the carriage. One footman would open the door while the other would let down the collapsible step, which was sometimes covered with the same velvet as that used for the coach lining. They would then stand to attention, with one arm stiffly extended, so that the ladies could cling on to it as they stepped down from the carriage, which could be as much as three feet off the ground, and which tilted over alarmingly at an angle of thirty degrees as they put their foot on the step, or even more if they were somewhat bulky.

44

In fashionable houses, footmen could be on duty until the early hours of the morning. If they fell asleep while they were out on the box, the coachman would draw the crop of his whip under the footman's nose to awaken him without arousing the suspicions of the mistress that James was drunk yet again. One footman, who had been working excessively long hours for a number of days, nodded off while he was on the box of a barouche and caused consternation, if no actual physical damage, among the lady passengers when he fell off the box backwards and landed in their laps. The outraged ladies accused him of being "tipsy", which was their normal explanation for any offending behaviour by their servants.[26] In older coaches, footmen had to stand on the hard undersprings which jolted violently. One Victorian coachbuilder claimed that this caused some of them "to spit blood, from violent and continued concussion", though it seems more likely that they were in the first stages of consumption owing to their poor living and working conditions.[27] Like members of the stable staff, footmen needed impeccable references to be employed in aristocratic households. Lady Walsingham used to ask the following questions when she was getting a reference about a footman from a former employer: Is he a good worker? Does he drink, swear or smoke? Is he honest, good-tempered and intelligent? Is he too fond of the maidservants? Is he clean in his habits? Does he smell?[28]

One indispensable servant in the richest, most pretentious, stables was the tiger, or miniature groom. The tiger came into fashion in Regency days when curricles were built with a small padded seat for the groom at the back of the carriage between the large C springs and continued with the cabriolet which had a little platform. The smartest men-about-town had the largest horses and the smallest tigers. "In shape and make," wrote G. N. Hooper, the Victorian coachbuilder, "he was a man in miniature, his proportions perfect, his figure erect and somewhat defiant; his coat fitted as if it had been moulded on him; his white buckskin breeches were spotless; his top-boots perfection; his hat, with its narrow binding of gold or silver lace, and brims looped up with gold or silver cord, brilliant with brushing, was worn jauntily."[29] The tiger, whose main function apart from ornament, was to hold the horse's head when his master left the carriage, survived throughout the nineteenth century into the cycling age, when the Prime Minister, the Marquis of Salisbury, found a new use for him at his home of Hatfield House, Hertfordshire. "His need of exercise drove him to trycycling when, in his declining years, long walks became too fatiguing. Then he had most of the paths in the nearer part of the park asphalted. For this recreation he used to wear a kind of sombrero hat and a special short sleeveless cloak with a hole in the middle, which,

A groom brings the dog cart to the front door for his master in the 1880s.

together with his greying beard, rather gave him the appearance of a cowled and hirsute monk. If he intended to ride up and down some of the more sloping paths he would order his under coachman to come with him. The young 'tiger' helped to push him up the hills, and then, coming down again, he would as often as not be told to 'jump up behind' and stand on the axle. The 'tiger' rested his hands on the Prime Minister's broad shoulders, and the two of them would sail downhill together with the front wheel rocking and zigzagging over the irregularities of the asphalt."[30] Lord Salisbury had always had a liking for speed. Earlier, in the Eighties, his famous seventeen-minute dashes in his brougham from Downing Street to King's Cross, where he caught the train for Hatfield, had provided an outlet for his sporting instincts.

Like the indoor servants, the stable staff had become expert in cheating their employers to supplement their low wages. Many coachmen once made a regular weekly profit by overcharging for axle grease which had to be used every eighty or hundred miles, though this source of income disappeared when Collinge's patent axles were introduced in the early years of the nineteenth century, as they only needed greasing every four or five thousand miles.[31] Stable servants also expected to receive commissions from coachbuilders, saddlers and harness manufacturers. Some dishonest servants were quite willing to accept hay and oats of an inferior quality if the corn chandler rewarded them sufficiently, even though this sometimes had disastrous effects on the horses' health.

Coachmen and grooms who sold one of their master's horses expected to receive a tip from the purchaser – their "reg'lars" as they called it – to seal the contract. These "reg'lars" usually amounted to only a few shillings, but there were much bigger profits to be made by dishonest coachmen when their kind-hearted employer instructed them to shoot an old horse to give it an abrupt, but dignified end to its life after years of loyal service. Many of these horses never died, in England anyway, but joined the long trail of ancient farm horses to the Continent, where they ended up on the dinner tables of the Belgians and the French who are less fastidious than most English people about eating horse meat. Others were sold to copers and gipsies.

One lady in the Midlands ordered her coachman to shoot a favourite mare which had already been pensioned off for a number of years. The coachman dug a grave in the grounds and the sad owner listened with compassionate feelings to the final, fatal shot. Some days after this merciful execution, her suspicions were aroused. They were confirmed when she ordered the grave to be opened and found it empty, Her coachman finally admitted that he had sold the horse. In another case, a clergyman instructed his coachman to shoot an old horse. The coachman's deception was only discovered some years later because horses, like elephants, have long memories. One day, the clergyman's son saw a gipsy thrashing a horse because it would not pass their gate. He ran outside to protest and recognized their old horse immediately.[32]

In addition to these exactions, stable staff had some recognized perquisites. The coachman had the right to claim the old wheels of a carriage if he had been in his master's employment as long as the wheels had been in use.[33] As a consequence, the coachman had a vested interest in ensuring by fair means or foul that the wheels wore out as quickly as possible. Many masters allowed their stable staff to retain their livery after it had been in use for a year. They had discovered by long experience that this was the only effective way of ensuring that their servants took good care of their expensive clothes. The servants sold their old liveries to second-hand clothes dealers, who exported them to Germany and Scandinavia where the facings were used to adorn the uniforms of minor officials. There were often unseemly squabbles in the stables between the valet, who had a reversionary interest in his master's clothes, and the stableboy, who was often given the job of cleaning the master's riding habit and boots, as the valet did not want his future perquisites to be damaged by some ignorant boy's clumsiness.

One of the grooms' perquisites affected the wider community and contributed greatly to the pollution of the capital in Victorian times. Instead of removing the dung from the mews every day, the grooms stacked it up until there was a sufficiently large load to sell to a market gardener for a shilling or so. As one writer in the *Medical Times* complained: "In some places there are dung pits containing the collectings of a fortnight's dung, which, when disturbed for removal, casts out an offensive effluvium, as sickening as it is disgusting to the whole neighbourhood ... Of this manure there are always (at a moderate computation) remaining daily in the mews and stable-yards of the metropolis, at least 2,000 cart-loads."[34] These dung heaps, and the great piles of horse droppings in every road, made Victorian cities a perfect breeding ground for flies, disease and smells, facts which we tend to forget when we look back on those days with nostalgia.

(Right above) *The town chariot of the Rothschild family built in about 1820.*

(Right below) *The Rothschild posting chariot, used for Continental travel, which was built at about the same time.*

4

THE GIG SET

"The first idea of a successful Englishman is either to mount on horseback, to give his wife a carriage, or to do both", wrote Sidney in his massive, quarto *Book of the Horse*, which was designed to teach the aspiring middle classes how to achieve both aims in the most successful and approved style.[1] Books of instruction proliferated as the new rich sought to learn the mysteries of driving, riding and carriage etiquette. "Madge" of *Truth*, who was always full of good advice, started sensibly with the basics. "Brougham", she proclaimed, should be pronounced "broom", quite short and monosyllabic. She realized that this might seem "a trifle" to some of her less devoted readers, but she warned them sternly that like "many another equally small matter, it is indicative of those accustomed to good society".[2] She had some further advice for those men who had hired a "broom" to take their ladies to the opera or the theatre to ensure that they could find their vehicle again in the crush of coaches and carriages at the end of the performance. "It is a miserable business on a wet night", she wrote, "to hunt for a brougham up and down ill-lighted streets when in evening dress and patent leather boots ... Nor do ladies enjoy waiting in the draughty vestibule of opera-house, theatre, or concert-room for an indefinite period while a short-sighted cavalier is groping about the streets for their carriage."[3] She advised these "cavaliers" to give the coachman a brightly-coloured handkerchief to wave when the crowds came out, though if her sensible advice had been too widely adopted it might well have increased the very confusion it was designed to cure.

Even if the "cavalier" found the right carriage, quickly and surely, his duties

(Left) *The ambition of every aspiring middle class lady was to have her own carriage and liveried groom.*

were by no means at an end, for it could sometimes be no less of a laborious task to "hand ladies to their carriage", particularly if the party included any sticklers for etiquette, which in Victorian times it would almost certainly have done. "Madge" told her readers that "a man offers his right arm to the senior of the party and walks with her to the door, opening it with his left hand. The others will probably follow without escort, but if not, he must offer it to each in turn, holding an umbrella over them should it be raining."[4] Propriety was no less important within the carriage. Any gentleman knew that it was obligatory for him to sit with his back to the horses, unless the lady invited him to join her on the front seat, which she would scarcely have done in that prurient age unless he was a relative and, sometimes, not even then. He also knew that it was mandatory for him to throw away his half-smoked cigar in a decorous but expensive gesture, as many ladies were even more strongly opposed than the anti-smoking brigade are at the present time to what one young Victorian miss in *Punch* called that "nasty, odious, dirty, filthy, disgusting and most objectionable habit".

When no "cavalier" was present, the youngest lady was expected to take the gentleman's or back seat, though she was assured by one casuistical member of the aristocracy that this "would be a matter of courtesy on her part, and not of etiquette".[5] The rules for two ladies getting out of a carriage, however, were governed by a stricter etiquette. "The hostess would descend after her guest, and not before her, unless it was more convenient to do otherwise, when she would make some polite remark before alighting." When two ladies were getting into a vehicle, the hostess would allow her lady friend to enter the carriage first, though "if a lady were merely calling on an acquaintance to take her for a drive", wrote the same member of the aristocracy, "she would not descend from her carriage for the purpose of allowing her to enter it before her".[6]

As ladies often went out in their carriages for general display rather than specific purpose, there were prescribed hours for their drives so that their equipages could be admired, or denigrated, by the greatest number of other ladies in similar idle circumstances. Outside London, the usual hours were 4 p.m. to 7 p.m. in the summer and 3 p.m. to 5 p.m. or even earlier in the winter. For those who drove themselves in a pony phaeton, midday to 2 p.m. was the most fashionable time in the Eighties.[7] In Victorian times, a picnic could take place at any hour of the day, but strict convention governed the journey to the selected site. Lady Colin

(Right) *In the leisured years of Queen Victoria's reign, people had much more time to indulge in social politeness in the streets.*

50

The working classes loved to ride out in a carriage, even if it was only to a Sunday school excursion.

Campbell warned her readers that it was far more becoming for members of a picnic party to travel in different conveyances, "some in carriages of various descriptions, large waggonettes being the pleasantest; some on horseback; some by boat, it may be; but never in a long procession, reminding one of the string of vans full of children, or members of various benefit clubs, going to Epping Forest or Bushey Park for the day, who wave their pocket handkerchiefs at each passer-by".[8] The new middle classes had to learn the old aristocratic trick of attracting attention to their privileged pleasures without seeming to do so. For many members of the middle classes who rarely travelled in any grander vehicle than a horse-drawn omnibus with straw scattered on the floor, most of this sound advice was largely academic; but they were so ambitious for better things that they liked to be prepared.

A very small minority of the middle classes could afford to be no less extravagant than the aristocracy in their carriage habits. With the great opportunities for making money in Victorian times, when income tax at its lowest point was only twopence in the £, some of the great speculators, financiers, engineers, cotton masters and brewers lived in just as grand a style and kept as many horses, carriages and servants as aristocrats did. Later in the reign, more of the second-generation new rich moved out into the countryside, where their dividends and dowries, and their pairs of well-matched bays with silver-plated harness, their liveried coachmen and their footmen and their grooms, made them formidable rivals in local tradesmen's eyes to the local squire. "They spend as much in a week," commented one shopkeeper in a small country town, "as the squire do in a month, and don't cheapen nothing, and your cheque just whenever you like to ask for it. That's what I call gentlefolks."[9] In the cities, and particularly in the capital, there were always some improvident intellectuals, such as Samuel Beazley, the architect and dramatist, who lived like lords without their capital. He once told a friend: "I have a carriage, and a cabriolet, and three horses, and a coachman and a footman, and a large house, and a cook and three maid-servants, and a mother and a sister – and half-a-crown."[10]

A few of the middle classes were no less eccentric than some aristocrats. The hypochondriac Victorian philosopher, Herbert Spencer, often ordered his coachman to stop in the middle of Regent Street or Piccadilly while he was out for his daily airing in his victoria so that he could investigate the state of his health. While he took his own pulse, he remained philosophically oblivious to the curses of other coachmen and the resulting traffic jam, as the vehicles could soon go on again while he could not, if his life was in suspected peril. "If the oracle proved favourable, the drive was continued; if not Mr. Spencer was driven home."[11] Mr. Richard and Mr. Walter Gladstone, unmarried nephews of the Liberal prime minister, were another pair of eccentrics. Although they lived together in a handsome Georgian mansion, they never made the daily journey to work together owing to the peculiarities of their domestic arrangements, but were driven each in his own carriage by his own coachman to the local railway station to catch separate trains to Liverpool. It was an inflexible house rule that Mr. Walter always had his breakfast first. After he had drunk his five gills of milk, which had to be warm from the cow and laced with three gills of rum, he left the table and went outside to enter his carriage. Mr. Richard then appeared for his breakfast which always consisted of nothing but potted shrimps.[12]

But these were all middle-class anomalies and exceptions. In the new horse-and-carriage suburbs which ringed each city, life was far more serious and respectable – if no less pretentious. Even before the railways had been built, some manufacturers and professional men had moved out to the inner suburbs, whence they commuted each day by horse and carriage. In the first quarter of the nineteenth century, they left central Liverpool for Southport, Hoylake and Aigburth; Manchester for Alderley Edge and Wilmslow; and Birmingham for New Hall and Edgbaston.[13] London carriage commuters moved out at a later date to such districts as Highgate, Putney, Wimbledon, Edmonton and Tottenham. In these suburbs, it was still possible in the Eighties to rent a large house with its own coach house and stable and an acre or so of land for about £150 a year. Even smaller villas often had their own stables. If not, a neighbour's could sometimes be rented or the horses might be kept at a livery and bait stable at the local inn, though this was more often done with hacks than harness horses.

The most admired middle-class carriage was the brougham. Ever since the first coach had been built in Britain, probably for the Earl of Rutland in 1555, the private, four-wheeled closed carriage had been the prerogative of the rich and powerful, until the brougham was introduced at the beginning of the Victorian age. The brougham was the first and greatest innovation of the new urban carriage age, providing a cheap middle-class substitute for the coach. It was much less expensive to buy and to run as it needed only one horse and could be driven by a coachman unaccompanied by any other servant, without attracting social scorn. The coachman's livery could be of the simplest. By the Eighties even trousers were socially permissible instead of expensive top boots. The brougham was equally suitable for town or country, for a single person or a whole family. "The social results of the brougham have been immense", enthused the author of an article in *All the Year Round* in 1866, "harmonizing families, bringing husband and wife together, accommodating children, making beauties look more beautiful, cutting off the necessity for a footman."[14] The brougham was extremely popular among doctors not only for its general utility and convenience but also for its use in attracting new patients, as some Victorians chose their doctor more for his carriage than his medical skills. One doctor who had a green brougham drawn by two fine grey horses found that "people who did not keep carriages themselves were particular in engaging him, because they liked to see his handsome vehicle parading before their houses".[15] In the country, the most desirable middle-class alternative to the brougham was the waggonette.

Some of the new rich, in their need to outdo the Joneses, tried to compensate for the smallness of their miniature brougham by hiring gigantic horses and coachmen, despite Sidney's advice that "there is nothing in worst taste . . . than a small brougham, a massive coachman and a gigantic footman in full liveries, and a pair of sixteen-hands barouche horses before them".[16] In that age when "to be smart and to look smart was then and for many years after the ambition of all those with

54

social aspirations", the middle classes would do almost anything respectable to attract the envious glances of their equally ignorant and unsophisticated neighbours.[17] The privilege of wearing the cockade which was reserved by right for servants of army and navy officers, members of the militia and volunteer forces, lord lieutenants, deputy lieutenants and high sheriffs, was being greatly abused by late Victorian times, as one member of the aristocracy lamented, so that many ambitious members of the middle classes added it, without authority, to their servants' livery.[18]

Although the brougham remained the most desirable carriage among the middle classes, comparatively few of them could afford to have one. In the Seventies, it cost only £50 or so a year to employ that essential triumvirate of indoor staff, consisting of a cook, a parlourmaid and a housemaid, but it needed about £300 or more a year to keep a stylish, circular-fronted brougham and a pair of horses in London with "your crest on its panels, well-matched horses, high steppers, good action (due to a stiff bit and a tight bearing-rein) a coachman in handsome livery, a cockade (you are not in H.M. service, but it doesn't matter), buckskins and picklejar boots".[19] To keep even the most unpretentious single-horse brougham with a groom in quiet sober livery cost about £200 a year in London, and to keep a waggonette and a horse in the country about £120.[20] In addition there was the initial cost of the horse, carriage and harness; the rent, possibly, of a coach house and stables; and a vast stock of stable equipment including a set of shoebrushes, three leathers, two sponges, a body brush, a curry comb, a spoke brush, two water brushes, a dandy brush, a carriage brush, a hood brush, a scraper, a mane comb, a trimming comb, a singeing lamp, a thermometer, a pair of scissors, a picker, two oil tins, a stable broom, a fork, a corn sieve, a shovel, a hair broom, a keg of olive oil soap, a steel burnisher, a stall brush, a box of boot-top powder, six white rubbers, six dusters, a pair of clogs, two bottles of blacking, wooden washing buckets, drinking buckets, and horse clothing.[21]

Faced with this daunting capital expenditure and the high annual running costs, most of the middle classes had to lower their sights to a less ambitious level and to make do with a one-horse, two-wheeled gig, a pony and trap or a donkey cart, all of which came in a remarkable variety of designs and quality. In the Eighties, a gig could be bought for £20 to £25 and pony for a little less. The annual tax at that time was only fifteen shillings for a two-wheeler against two guineas for

(Overleaf) *Carriages drawn up outside Marlborough House after a function there in 1891 during the London season.*

a four-wheeled carriage.[22] And they were much cheaper to run as a gig could be looked after by a gardener-groom earning £30 or so a year.

The gig or trap was by far the most common carriage. In 1864 no less than half of the 272,466 carriages in the country were one-horse, two-wheeled vehicles.[23] No suburban villa could be considered complete without its gig-house and its gardener-groom, public evidence that the master had joined the carriage-owning set, even if it should be for only a brief period, as many gigs were so "frequently driven by those who could neither afford the Money to support them, nor the Time spent in using them" that one Lord Chief Justice called them "bankrupt carts".[24] Nevertheless, the middle classes continued to revere them, bowing down before "an empty go-cart, that costs, perhaps, a hundred and fifty pounds a year; while they ... pity the wretched superstitions of the Hindoos".[25] At a murder trial in Hertfordshire in the 1820s one witness solemnly declared his belief that the accused must have been respectable because he kept a gig!

Although the proud owner of a gig may have gained the respect if not the affection of his gig-less neighbours, he often lost out in most other ways by getting the worst of everything in the carriage world: the most dangerous vehicles, the worst horses and screws, and the most incompetent servants. Two-wheelers were far more dangerous than carriages with four wheels, as if the horse fell, the shafts went down to the ground with the animal, sometimes catapulting the occupants to injury or death over the horse's head. There was an old saying among coachmen that "half the coachmen were killed out of gigs".[26] Many members of the middle classes, particularly women, bought mares for harness because they were cheaper than geldings, though the long-term costs might wipe out the initial saving. The author of that runaway best-selling book, *Caveat Emptor* or *The Adventures of a Gentleman in Search of a Horse*, warned his readers that no dependence could be placed on mares: "they may be temperate and steady for months, or even years, and yet when the season arrives, will kick your chaise to pieces".[27] Members of the middle classes who wanted to save a pound or two by getting a horse for a bargain price were the favourite victims of the many crooked Victorian horse dealers, or copers, who knew dozens of tricks to make an old screw appear youthful again, such as carefully painting the grey hairs with Indian ink, which was guaranteed to take years off the looks of any old dark-coloured horse – until it rained.

Their stable servants were often as deceptive and decrepit as their horses. Not even the lowest groom from any aristocratic stable would have designed to work for a one-gig family, so that the majority of the middle classes had to be content with some unskilled local lad or incompetent, drunken gardener-groom. Most

58

Victorians did know something about horses as even many city-dwellers had recent connections with the countryside where, until 1851, the majority of people had lived; but many people imagined that they knew more than they actually did. In the country, young lads were taken straight from the plough and after a few years' experience of cleaning harness, washing carriages and grooming horses, were dignified with the title of coachman or groom.[28] Joseph Arch, who led the first successful national farm labourers' strike in the early 1870s, started work as a crow-scarer at the age of nine for fourpence a day, and progressed, within three years to the post of ploughman. "There was a wealthy banker and Justice of Peace in the village," he wrote, "a great hunting man, who kept six or seven horses. I began to drive a pair of horses at plough for him; and, after a bit, thinking I suppose that I was a smart, likely lad, he took me into his stables."[29] But Arch had other ambitions and left after a few years. One young Victorian lad who remained in service for a much longer time was Henry White, who was born at Bagendon near Cirencester, where his father was an odd-job man. At the age of fifteen, in the same year that Queen Victoria came to the throne, he was given the post of groom and coachman to a local rector, who also expected him to wait at table, to clean the knives and boots, to do a little gardening, and to make himself generally useful in his spare time! In keeping with the magnificence of his employer's carriage – a humble donkey cart – Henry was fitted out with a hand-made livery consisting of buckled shoes, white silk stockings, plush breeches, a brilliant brimstone-coloured waistcoat, and a sky-blue coat embroidered with two rows of gold braid and decorated with a set of bright gilt buttons, which would not have disgraced a coachman on the box of an aristocratic barouche.[30]

Only the meanest, or the most indigent, members of the middle classes tried to make do with a juvenile man-of-all-work. More commonly they employed a gardener-groom or a self-professed coachman, who was expected to be able to turn out a horse and carriage in reasonable condition for one daily journey five or six days a week, a feat of which most of them were not usually incapable unless they had stored up their daily ration of free beer or had raided their master's cellar again. Mary Paley Marshall, who lived in the country rectory where she had been born from 1850 to 1870, remembered that her father employed a man called Richard Hoggard who did "all the work of a large garden, and looked after the horse and pony. He now and then got drunk. Once he was found harnessing the horse with its head where its tail should be, and when remonstrated with said 'Some folks likes it one way, and some another.'"[31] Drunkenness was just as much the curse of coachmen as of the working classes in Victorian times!

Most of the middle classes were as kind to their horses as their pockets, or their ignorance, would permit. One gentleman left £50 a year in his will for a favourite black mare to be "properly and comfortably kept in some park or paddock" and to have her shoes taken off and never to be ridden or harnessed again.[32] Every year, more people were usually imprisoned for cruelty to horses than for causing deaths or injuries to people in road accidents. In 1862–3, for example, the Royal Society for the Prevention of Cruelty to Animals, prosecuted 735 people for ill-treating horses and of these nearly 150 were sent to prison or committed for not paying fines.[33] At about the same time less than a hundred people were sent to prison each year in the great cities for causing deaths and injuries in traffic accidents.

Many of the lads and men employed by the middle classes in their stables were totally unfitted by both temperament and lack of training to be in charge of horses. The real-life sufferings of harness horses in Victorian times were sometimes far worse than those experienced by Ginger and the eponymous hero of *Black Beauty*, that haunting children's classic published originally as an adult book by Anna Sewell in 1877. A horse travelling with unaccustomed speed on some unusually urgent journey, might not have been propelled by natural zest, but because it had been figged up by the coachman who had stuffed some ginger into its anus. Victorian newspapers were full of stories about atrocities committed by half-witted stable boys and bad-tempered grooms. In 1866, John Powell, "a morose-looking boy stated to be fifteen years of age" was prosecuted for torturing, maiming and slaying a horse by forcing a stick into its anus and holding burning paper under its nostrils until it died of "frightful internal injuries" in the greatest agony. He was sentenced to two years' hard labour.[34]

There were far fewer newspaper reports about gentlemen's cruelty to horses as it was one of the main axioms of the Victorian age that any man who could commit such dastardly acts could be no gentleman. Nevertheless, some gentlemen did. The Royal Society for the Prevention of Cruelty to Animals, to its great credit, did bring some prosecutions against a number of gentlemen, but magistrates were usually reluctant to convict a member of their own class. The society instituted a prosecution of Mr. John Donithorne Taylor, "a gentleman of considerable property" at Southgate, Middlesex, who had kept a horse without food or water for six days as a punishment, but the case was dismissed. Some months later the society tried again by bringing another case against Taylor for being cruel to his pony.

The prosecution said that while Taylor was out driving with his daughter, the pony swerved and turned towards the gate of a house which his daughter was in

The gig was the most widely owned middle-class carriage.

the habit of visiting. "Mr. Taylor immediately struck it with his whip; the poor animal reared, upon which he commenced beating it, causing the pony to plunge and kick until it released itself from the vehicle. Mr. Taylor then got down, and, gathering up the reins in his left hand, close to the pony's head, commenced beating it about the head in the most cruel manner with the butt end of the whip. He continued his brutal treatment for about a quarter of an hour, till the pony trembled from head to foot with agony."

When his daughter pleaded with him not to be so cruel, he turned to her, like a wicked father in some Victorian melodrama, and shouted, "Damn your eyes, you are as bad as the pony", though he retained sufficient self-control not to play out his part by using the horsewhip on her.

In court, an unrepentant Taylor said that the pony needed a good thrashing with a stout ash stick three or four hours a day. The magistrates rather reluctantly fined him £2, but refused to grant costs to the society.[35]

When both the master and his servant were involved in a case of cruelty to a horse, the magistrates were far more likely to convict the latter. In 1856, William George Craven, a lieutenant in the 1st Life Guards, and his groom, George

Belcher, were charged with having caused the death of a 200-guinea horse by driving it too fast. The lieutenant, it was stated, had driven his dog cart at speeds of up to 17 m.p.h. in a race to catch a train he had just missed at Windsor station. When the horse arrived at Hounslow, it was trembling, exhausted and so "blown" from its thirteen-mile gallop that it could eat no corn but only drink a pint of gruel. The unfortunate groom was left with the task of taking it back to Windsor. He waited for an hour before he set out, and stopped again after two-and-a-half miles, but the horse died in a livery and bait stable at Egham. The magistrates were divided in their opinion of the lieutenant's guilt and dismissed the case against him; but the groom was convicted and fined the maximum amount of £5.[36]

Aristocrats, some of whom had a much greater respect and liking for horses than for human beings, were often sterner avengers of cruelty wherever it was found. The Duke of Portland once ordered his coachman to chase another carriage, in which the coachman had been furiously whipping his horses. When the coachman was caught, the duke had him arrested; but he did not proceed with the charge after his master, Lord Windsor, decided to dismiss him.

The sixth Earl of Essex was equally infuriated when he was strolling along Bond Street one afternoon and saw a coachman savagely whipping one of a pair of bays in a sociable landau. He ran across the street and said: "By George, if you dare to flog the horse in that way, I'll pull you off your box, put you in the hands of the police, and complain to your master!" By that time, as was usual on such occasions, the incident had attracted a number of bystanders, some of whom were indignantly crying out "Shame! Shame!"

Lord Essex demanded to know the owner's name, but the coachman refused to tell him. The earl, a man of strong principles, whose family motto was *fide et fortitudine* (faith and courage), then climbed resolutely into the carriage and said he intended to remain there until the coachman gave him the name, which, eventually, he did. The coachman was later charged with cruelty, with the Earl of Essex giving evidence against him, and the magistrate, doubtless in some awe of the earl's rank, sentenced the coachman to a month's hard labour.[37] But neither aristocratic vigilance nor the efforts of the Royal Society for the Prevention of Cruelty to Animals was ever able to bring an end to such public brutality. Throughout Victorian and Edwardian times, groups of shocked bystanders gathered at similar scenes to raise their little voices of protest against this cruelty, which was just one of the prices that society, and even more the unfortunate horses, had to pay for its old-fashioned means of urban transport.

5

HORSE DEALERS AND COPERS

To be a good judge of a horse was no gambler's sport or enthusiastic amateur's ambition in Victorian times, but a serious necessity which could save hundreds of pounds or even life itself. If Sir Robert Peel, the founder of the modern Conservative party, had only been as skilful at Tattersall's as he sometimes was in the House of Commons, he might not have died prematurely; but he preferred to let Lord Ossington choose a riding horse for him at auction and to ignore his own coachman's advice that the horse was likely to shy. Two months later, Sir Robert, who was one of the worst horsemen who ever graced, or disgraced, Rotten Row, was out riding in the Park when his horse was frightened by the sight of one of Lady Dover's daughters and threw Sir Robert over its head. He was taken by carriage to his house in Whitehall Gardens and died in agony some days later on a hydraulic bed.[1]

Horse dealing was at the heart of Victorian life. Every city, town and village had its own collection of horsy characters who congregated at dealers' yards, auction rooms, country fairs, particular inns and other places where the talk always came straight from the horse's mouth and every person always had some knowledge of a better bargain. Long years of riding and of driving had left its mark on their bodies, manifested in the rounded left wrist of the driver, the bandy legs of the former groom and the stiff gait of the ex-coachman who had spent so many years on the box. The whip, or ash switch, which they applied as ceaselessly to their own boots as they did at other times to the flanks of horses was as much a sign of their calling as the piece of wool in the shepherd's hat at the great hiring fairs for agricultural labourers which were held throughout the countryside every autumn. Their clothes were equally revealing of their former trades: the long postboy's greatcoat reaching to the ankles with half-a-dozen mother o' pearl buttons on the lapels matching those on the breeches; a loose fustian stable jacket, buttonless, and with the elbows peeping through; a jacket with multi-coloured patches. Their clothes had come straight from the stables and still bore the smell.

Most horse dealers were reputable men, but some were copers who practised every trick of their dishonest trade to deceive the ignorant and the gullible, amongst whom clergymen and old ladies were often predominant. A frisky, lively horse, which might become a runaway, was given what copers called the "ginger" – a sound thrashing for a few minutes to make it appear quiet and manageable – before it was displayed to the intended victim with soft and soothing words. If, on the other hand, the horse was nothing but a dull jade, the coper had another stratagem to make it temporarily regain the lost vigour and energy of its youth. The horse would be confined in a dark stall and would be released only when the client arrived, when it would bound out, startled, into the bright light with its head almost tossing and its knees almost bending. If the potential purchaser still retained some doubts about the horse's age, the coper could often clinch the deal by offering to show the horse's teeth, for even the most ignorant person then knew that the black marks, or infundibula, on the crowns of the incisor teeth gave a rough indication of age as they had disappeared in practically all horses by the age of nine. The coper would open the horse's mouth to reveal as regular and an impressive a set of marks as might ever be seen, though a closer examination would have revealed that they lacked the ring of pearly enamel surrounding genuine marks as they had just been burnt in by the coper with caustic or a hot iron in an operation which they, wittily, called "bishoping".[2]

If a horse was lame in one leg, the coper would restore nature's balance by making it lame in the other leg, too, so that the inexpert eye would be deceived into thinking that both legs were sound. This was achieved by hammering in a little stone, called a "pea" or a "plug", between the shoe and the most sensitive part of the hoof from which a small sliver had been removed. Lameness could also be temporarily disguised by soaking the leg in water or keeping it in clay. Blemished knees were stained to conceal the fault; lean horses were temporarily fattened with a surfeit of unwholesome food; and broken-winded horses could be given a transient soundness by keeping them short of water or food or by giving them

(Right) *The blacksmith was one of the essential supports of the carriage world. This mid-nineteenth-century painting by Landseer is entitled* Blacksmith Shoeing the Bay Mare.

antimony, mashes of linseed, or grease dumplings.[3] Copers became so expert in their deceptive art that one man actually bought "the self-same nag for a buggy horse that he himself had sold (the animal having broke down in a contest for the Coventry plate) only the season before". The metamorphosis was accomplished by means of "a muriatic-made star in the forehead, docking, hogging and clipping".[4]

Copers usually sold their horses through beguiling advertisements appealing to the compassion, the snobbery, or the greed of their intended victims. Phrases such as "price not so much an object as a good master", "a property of a nobleman going abroad" or "sold by order of the executors of a deceased clergyman" were, almost invariably, indications that a coper was at work. Newspapers and sporting journals were full of copers' advertisements such as the following:

> Splendid match pair of bay geldings for Sale, 15.1 (hands) high, ages five and six off, on short legs, and a perfect model of a cart-horse in growth, with much quality combined; very fast, with good knee action, small head, good neck, and broad chest and thighs; are pure Welsh breed, and worthy of the notice of a gentleman and others wanting horses for riding and driving; both warranted good hunters, up to heavy weight, quiet in any kind of harness, valuable to a timid person, no vice or blemish, and of a kind, good temper; suitable for brougham or victoria or a light landau; no day too long, no distance too far. For trial.[5]

The victim would take the horses on trial, leaving half the purchase price as a deposit, but would soon return them when he discovered that they were kickers, or lame, or had some other fault or vice. On returning to the stables, he would find only an apologetic groom, who took the horses and promised faithfully that the owner, who happened to be at dinner or otherwise engaged, would come round that very night with the deposit. He never did, and when the victim went back to the stables again, he found nothing but a "To Let" sign outside.[6] Victorian copers made thousands of pounds out of the "vanishing owner" trick.

In London, owners could gain some protection from copers by taking out a two-guinea annual subscription to the Royal Veterinary College in Camden

(Left above) *The old Tattersall's as seen by Cruikshank in the 1820s.*

(Left below) *Tattersall's moved to enlarged premises in London in 1865. This photograph shows potential customers inspecting carriages there in about 1895.*

Town, the A.A. of the horsy world. Subscribers could obtain a free examination of up to five horses a year. The mere mention of the college's name was often sufficient to betray the coper, as none of them would ever agree to send their horses there for an inspection on the pretext that the college's vets knocked horses about. There were also a number of veterinary surgeons or horse doctors in all big towns and cities, the best-known in London having their surgeries in the Bond Street area, like Mr. Mavor in Bond Street itself, Mr. Dollar in New Bond Street, and Mr. Field in Oxford Street, while horse dentists tended to congregate in St. Martin's Lane.

The veterinary world was not free from dishonesty in Victorian times. Some vets acted in collusion with disreputable dealers to cheat breeders by providing the dealer with a certificate of unfitness for a horse which had been purchased in the country, so that the breeder was forced to remit half of the agreed purchase price. But there was more misjudgment than dishonesty. Even reputable vets could make mistakes from time to time as the horse is a strong-willed, complex animal with many potential vices and subject to many different ailments and afflictions, some of which also affect human beings. These include bone spavin (an infection of the bones of the hock joint); bronchitis; cataract; corns; coughs; dropsy; enlarged glands; enlarged hock; glanders (swellings below the jaw); acute founder or inflammation of the foot; lampas (a swelling in the roof of the mouth); liver disease; mallenders and sallenders (a scurfy eruption at the bend of the knee in the fore and hind legs respectively); mange; nasal gleet (a discharge from the nose); poll evil (a head ulcer); ringworm; sand crack (a crack in the hoof); warts; the yellows (jaundice); and many respiratory diseases of the lungs, windpipe and throat, including wheezing, whistling and roaring. In addition horses can acquire numerous vices such as biting, bolting, jibbing; kicking; rolling in stables; shying; shivering; star-gazing; and weaving.[7] Even in the best-managed stables a vicious horse could sometimes break loose at night and long before the groom had had time to stumble down the dark stairs the leg of another horse might be broken or the neck of another be one large mass of raw flesh.

Rogue horses were far more common in Victorian times than they are now. Vices were often caused by the mistreatment of some ignorant, drunken or malicious stable boy or groom. A pretence of biting, which had been playfully encouraged for the stable lad's amusement in the horse's youth could become an established, vicious habit in maturity. Jibbing was often the result of bad breaking. Roaring was far more prevalent among large horses, for as Col. Maude, the Secretary to the Master of the Horse, was forced to confess: "We hardly ever have

Big horse fairs were held every year in many market towns. This one took place at Horncastle, Lincolnshire, in 1864.

an instance of a harness horse 15.3 hands becoming a roarer, whereas almost all the big bays end by being roarers."[8] But so great was the desire to show off to one's friends by trying to emulate royalty that many people brought trouble to their stables and creditors to their doors by using unnecessarily large horses.

The safest, but not the least expensive, way of obtaining a sound horse was by going to reputable dealers, who were to be found in all large towns and cities in Victorian and Edwardian times. First-class London dealers guaranteed that their horses were sound and free from any vice. They would also change any horse that proved to be unsuitable, though they charged their normal hiring fee of twelve guineas a month in the season and eight guineas at other times for the period that it had been in use. Their horses lived in luxurious stables, bedded in clean straw to their knees, and attended by a multitude of grooms, or strappers, many of whom were casual workers who could be hired for a few shillings a day then. There was highly-polished brass and leather everywhere. The customers could study the horse's action, before it was harnessed to a carriage, on a ride of bright red sand or straw in the partially-covered yard.

Some wealthy aristocrats, like Lord Michelham, preferred to have horses brought to their front door for their inspection, rather than visiting the dealer's yard. One of the dealer's staff would drive the horse and break back and forth in the street outside, while my lord observed the action from an upstairs window. Occasionally, a stable tout would obtain advance news of the impending demonstration and sell his knowledge for a small fee to a rival dealer, who would give his own unsolicited show in the street at the same time. Other lords were happy to leave the buying of their carriage horses to their head coachman or agent, who were expert whips with excellent connections in the trade. On November 28, 1852, Alexander Brown, the agent to the Earl of Egmont, wrote to his employer:

> Fearing the second horse is too hot and firey (*sic*) a worker for the other and hoping to see another tomorrow that may possibly suit better, I shall be glad if your Lordship will delay sending to Dorking till I write again. I am unwilling to return this horse if I cannot meet with a better as he is not dear.

It didn't take him long to discover a better match, for on December 1, he wrote again:

> I have bought another horse today rising four for £23 subject to a trial tomorrow, Friday. If he suits, I will send the two on Monday morning.[9]

Dealers usually bought their horses as four-year-olds and broke them to harness in the city where they would be employed. Early every morning in Victorian times, Piccadilly was crowded with dealers' breaksmen, training new horses in a skeleton break, a vehicle consisting of a frame with no body-work and only a high box seat at the front and a platform at the back for the groom who could jump off quickly in any emergency. The newcomer was put into harness with a trained and trusted horse called a "schoolmaster", who would sometimes give its younger partner a savage nip on the neck if it wasn't learning fast enough.

In the thin light of dawn there were many fierce battles of will between breaksmen and their horses. Horace Smith recalls how he once bought a magnificent chestnut Hackney in Yorkshire for a large sum of money; but it would always lie down and refuse to budge when it was put into harness with another horse. Smith decided that more than one schoolmaster was needed to teach such a recalcitrant pupil. After bandaging the horse's legs and putting on kneecaps to make sure that it could not damage itself, Smith put it in a coach with three

68

schoolmasters, but the horse lay down again. "I proceeded to get up on the coach, with my friend still stretched out, and after a further look round to see that my harness was in order – and I had seen to it that it was all of the very strongest material, tough enough to pull half-a-dozen coaches – I gave instructions to let the other three horses walk on.

"My friend, who was still stubborn and obstinate, was dragged along the ground for some distance. Then I pulled up, and he jumped to his feet of his own accord, and never tried to lie down again. He had found his master, and proved to be one of the best harness horses I have ever driven."[10]

Patience, skill and experience are all necessary in breaking in a horse, but above all a firm conviction, in Smith's own words, that "horses must always be kept subservient and obedient to the wishes of their master".[11] There was no magic formula, but from time to time some charlatan or a genuine expert would appear, who claimed to have found one. One of the most spectacular demonstrations of skill, which astonished the whole of the horsy world, was given by John S. Rarey, who had been born in Grovetown, Ohio, on a visit to England in 1858. After he had broken in Lord Dorchester's thoroughbred stallion, Cruiser, which had been pronounced "an untameable devil", he went on to tame a zebra at the Zoo.[12] Rarey offered to teach a thousand people the secrets of his skill for a fee of ten guineas each, and he was soon over-subscribed when Queen Victoria and Prince Albert became two of his pupils after seeing a demonstration at Windsor Castle. His methods were merely a refinement of current practices. Rarey would make a vicious horse powerless with leg straps and hobbles and then bring it gently to its knees, repeating the process time after time until he had gained mastery; but none of his pupils ever rivalled him as they did not possess his unique, instinctive knowledge of a horse's mind and spirit.

Horse dealing was a risky business. "There's a horse," a big dealer once said, "by which I shall lose two hundred pounds. I gave two hundred pounds for him as a four-year, and expected to make at least three hundred by him as a hunter. He had the influenza, and when I began to get him into condition he made a noise, so, as he was no use for hunting, I ordered him to be broken to harness. The first time he was put in the break he threw himself down, blemished his hocks and broke his tail; so now he's barely worth twenty pounds."[13] It could also be a dangerous trade, particularly if you were unfortunate enough to have as one of your best customers some drunken daredevil like John Mytton of Halston, Shropshire, who never consumed less than four bottles of port a day and died of *delirium tremens* in Calais, where he had sought refuge from his creditors after squandering his vast

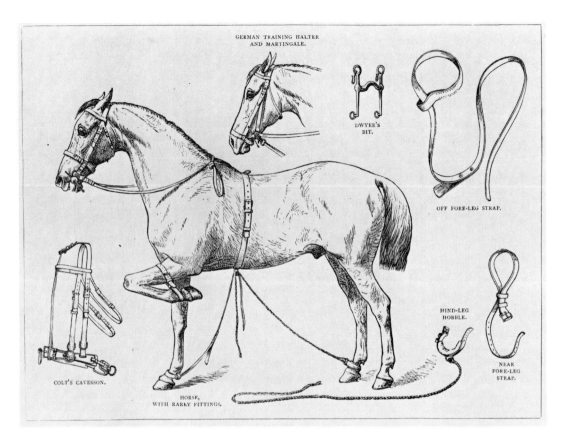

An illustration from Cassell's Book of the Horse.

fortune. He once bought a carriage horse from a dealer called Clarke in Meole Brace, Shropshire, and asked if it would make a good jumper. Clarke expressed some doubt. "We'll try him," said Mytton, promptly putting the horse in a gig. Giving the horse its head, he drove at a furious speed towards a closed turnpike gate, leaving the gig smashed up on one side, and the horse, the dealer and himself floundering on the road on the other.[14] Even without these imposed adventures, all dealers had some accidents from time to time, though very few had as many as George Talkington of Uttoxeter, Staffordshire. In the course of his long working life his injuries included a broken right shoulder; a fractured skull; three broken ribs on the left side; three broken ribs on the right side; a serious back injury; the right kneecap kicked off; a dislocation of the left ankle; seven ribs broken on the left and right sides; another serious back injury; two ribs and the breast bone broken; a

70

dislocation of the right shoulder; seven ribs broken yet again; a dislocation of the left shoulder and a broken arm; and two ribs broken and serious bruising to the thigh. But he had great virility and stamina, siring no less than eighteen children in fifteen years, and died not of any injury, but through natural causes when he was eighty-three years of age.[15]

All dealers had their ups and downs, both physically and financially, partly because many of their customers had an aristocratic aversion to paying their bills on time. But on the whole, with the great rises in the prices of carriage horses, dealers prospered in Victorian times. At the beginning of the reign, a good carriage horse could be bought for £25 to £30, but by the Seventies, £80 was a more normal price. A well-matched pair would have cost very much more. Joshua East, of Willesden, one of the biggest jobmasters in the capital who always had a thousand carriage horses for hire, told an official inquiry in 1873: "If you told me that you would give me £400 for a pair of carriage horses that you dare put your wife behind, a pair of nice, good horses, worth £200, and gave me a fortnight to get them in, I would not guarantee to buy them. I do not think there is a man in London that could do it."[16] Although dealers had to pay more themselves for unbroken horses, their profits rose proportionately. By the end of the reign it was not impossible for a dealer to make £600 or £700 on a pair of perfectly-matched carriage horses selling at £1,000.

Suitable horses became increasingly difficult to find, partly through lack of foresight and the English fashion of using geldings in carriage work. At the end of the road coaching era, some of the best mares had been bought by dealers on the Continent, where they were used for carriage work and could then be used for breeding when they came out of harness; but this was impossible in England where the best harness horses were all geldings. When they were old or injured, they went to the knacker's yard, a cab proprietor's yard, or, very occasionally, to the seaside where they hauled the bathing machines in and out of the sea. A further shortage of mares was caused by the export of large numbers for use as cavalry chargers during the Franco-Prussian war.

Horses from France, Germany, Hungary, Austria, Italy and the Netherlands were increasingly used in Victorian times to draw English carriages, even though most people continued to believe that they did not possess the stamina of English breeds. Imports of horses increased sixfold between 1862 and 1882, though not all of those were carriage horses.[17] By the beginning of the Nineties, Tattersall's, the best-known of the great London auction houses, was selling harness horses from the United States at eighty to 120 guineas each. Their regular Monday sales throughout the year, and the Thursday sales in the season, attracted not only the big London dealers and jobmasters but also an immense "throng of carriages, cabs, horses, grooms and tigers" to their new premises at Albert Gate, where they had moved from Grosvenor Place, at the back of St. George's Hospital, in 1865.[18] There, in a covered yard, with its lofty glass-roofed hall as big as a railway station, which had cost £30,000 to build, some of the best riding and driving horses in the kingdom were displayed, while in the adjacent gallery, behind an arched and columned screen, carriages for auction were also shown in all their highly-polished perfection.

Horse auctions were a regular weekly feature of town life in Victorian and Edwardian times. Some of the other big auctions in London were held by Rymill's in the Barbican, Ward's in the Edgware Road, the Park Lane Company in Park Lane and Piccadilly, and Alridge's in St. Martin's Lane, which was then virtually monopolized by saddlers and by dentists, some of whom treated human beings, and others horses. Most big provincial cities such as Reading, Rugby, Leicester and Swindon all had their own auctions in that age when the horse remained one of the main means of transport, as it had been ever since it was first domesticated, probably in north-west Asia, about four thousand years ago.

6

CARRIAGES — FOR SALE OR HIRE

Coachbuilding reached its peak of perfection in the Victorian age. Traditionalists, like Mr. V. Kesterton of Holland's, the Oxford Street coachbuilders, might mourn the passing of the perch, the heavy wooden beam which joined the two axles in old coaches. "A coach without a perch," he said disparagingly, "is no coach at all, only a four-wheel carriage."[1] But the replacement of the perch by elliptical leaf springs not only gave a smoother ride, but also made town coaches more man-oeuvrable by reducing the turning circle. Conservative lords might yearn for the good old days when the vehicles of fellow-peers were all painted in the family colours: "the Russell brown and blue, the Rutland and Sefton light yellow, the Hamilton red, the Foley reddish brown, the Harrington dark brown, the Anglesey dark yellow"; but commoners' usurpation of these aristocratic colours for their own use added a touch of warm, colourful pageantry to the city streets.[2] Old coachbuilders, like Mr. J. Philipson, a former president of the Institute of British Carriage Manufacturers, who had been in the trade for forty-five years, might despise the new-fangled methods of making springs, wheels and axles by sub-contract so that "coachmaking in some places appears to consist of little more than assembling the various parts together"; but mass production of some basic parts helped to keep carriage prices lower than they might otherwise have been and brought new prosperity to the trade.[3] He was equally contemptuous of the new class of owner who no longer had a carriage built to his individual and precise specifications. "Today," Philipson wrote in 1897, "the average carriage user chooses a finished vehicle as it stands in the showroom; it may be the shape of the body, or the colour of the painting, or the style of the trimming, which pleases his eye and determines his selection. He is seldom, very seldom, a judge of quality."[4]

Although there were more complaints in Victorian times about rattling windows, defective locks, leaky roofs and "a certain buzzing noise in the work of

J. OFFORD,

Coachbuilder,

79, WELLS STREET, OXFORD STREET,

AND 28, BROOK STREET, GROSVENOR SQUARE, LONDON.

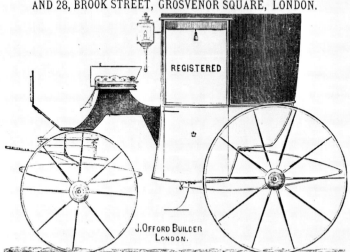

MEDICAL BROUGHAM.

This elegant Carriage is hung on a novel plan, by which the fore-wheels are brought within 30 inches of the hind ones, so that the draught is about half that of the ordinary brougham, and the saving to the horse immense. Measure your carriages and note the difference. From 120 guineas.

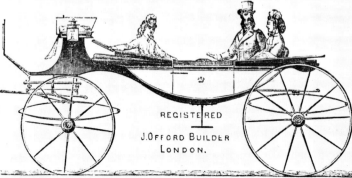

CANOE LANDAU.

With the patent Presto Self-acting Head which can be Opened by the Riders as easily as a Parasol. It is so simple that it cannot get out of order, and is no addition either to weight or price. Made in all shapes and sizes. Any Carriage can be hung with Offord's India-rubber Blocks, which prevent noise and shaking. A large, well-seasoned Stock of both New and Second-hand Carriages of all kinds for Sale, Hire, or Exchange. Good Second-hand Carriages wanted.

Coachmaker to the United States Ministers for 12 Years.

inferior makers", workmanship generally remained at a high level.[5] The English carriage, like Sheffield steel, retained its world-wide reputation for strength, quality and durability. Skilled craftsmen had adequate time during their long working week to take a pride in their work, more often at their own cost than their employer's as they were generally paid miserably low wages. Frank Clark, who worked for Windover's of Huntingdon before the First World War, recalls that he used to start work at 6 a.m. and finish at 6 p.m., with only half-an-hour for breakfast and an hour for dinner, five days of the week, and from 6 a.m. to 4 p.m. on Saturdays. "Take all the time you like within reason," his employers used to tell him, "just make a good job of it."[6]

Bodymakers, the aristocrats of the trade, earned the highest wages; but as they were usually piece workers they were not always employed for every week in the year. Carriage makers, who built the chassis, were the next highest paid craftsmen, earning about £2 to £3 a week. But only half of that wage was earned by the many other craftsmen involved in the building of a carriage: the blacksmiths who made all the iron work; the wheelwrights; the spring makers; the platers; the brace makers; the painters; the curriers who produced all the leather fittings; the trimmers who made the linings of cloth, satin, silk and velvet and the blinds of silk, taborette and morocco. In those days when more men were their own masters, carriage-making provided work for other skilled freelances, such as heraldic painters who painted the miniature crests, coats of arms and family mottoes on the carriage panels by the technique known as pouncing. The design was drawn on paper; the outline was perforated with a pin; and it was then transferred to the panels by dusting the paper with finely-powdered chalk or charcoal. One of the best-known heraldic painters in London was S. Cass of Hensbridge Place, Ordnance Road, St. John's Wood, who left two pattern books of the work he had done between 1828 and 1862.[7] It cost about £15 to have armorial bearings painted on a carriage in the middle of the reign.[8]

Coachbuilders scoured the forests of the world to obtain the best timber for their carriages. English ash, which is tough, light and easily bent, was invariably used for the framework; Honduras mahogany for the panels; American ash for the footboards; Jamaican lancewood for the shafts; American pine for the roof; Canadian or American hickory for the wheels; and English oak for the spokes. At the beginning of the reign, the wheel timber was often left in running water for two

(Left) *An advertisement which was produced by one of the big London coachbuilders.*

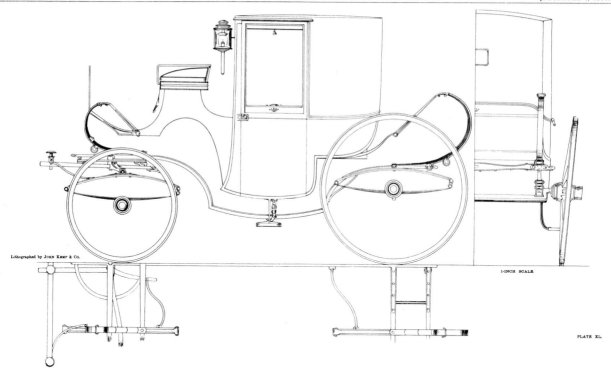

Lithographed by JOHN KEMP & CO.

1-INCH SCALE

PLATE XL.

A working drawing of a curved pattern single brougham, published in a trade journal.

months to toughen it in the old traditional way before it was seasoned; but by the end of the reign, many wheels were being imported ready made from the United States, where automatic lathes were capable of turning out 270 spokes an hour.[9] Before the carriage was painted it was tested by loading it with workmen who jumped up and down to test the chassis and swayed it from side to side. This precaution was always taken before Queen Victoria went out in one of her carriages.

The glossy, mirror-like surface of the painted panels was achieved by means of a painstaking process which could involve the application of up to twenty coats of primer, paint and varnish. "To the original smoothed wood would be given some four coats of a first colour mixed with japan and turpentine, each succeeding coat containing a little less japan and a little more turpentine; next came as many coats of grounding, composed of powdered ochre, turpentine and japan, and the stopping of any minute crevices or marks in the panels with white lead and gold size. This surface, when hard, was rubbed down with pumice-stone and water to perfect

76

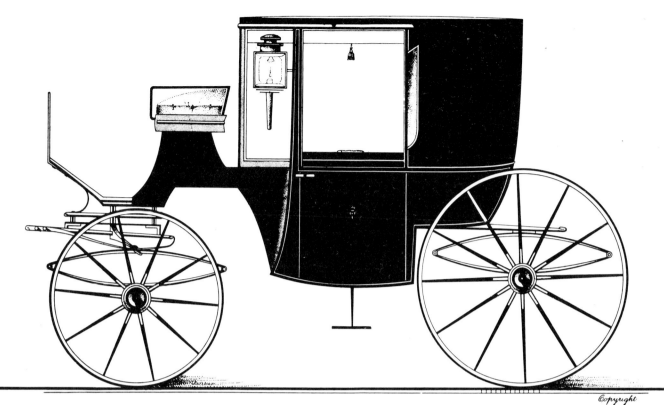

Copyright

An illustration from the Coach Builders, Harness Makers and Saddlers Art
Journal *showing the design of a brougham.*

smoothness in preparation for the priming, or preliminary painting in a colour
suited to the shade of the eventual surface. Some three coats of priming were usual,
each in turn when dry being smoothed off with sandpaper. The body paint or
ultimate colour was then put on in any number of coats – as many as were needed
to produce a completely clear and unclouded surface – sandpaper being used
between each. The next stage was the varnishing, at least six coats of fine copal
being given, and all but the final one rubbed down with powdered pumice applied
on a cloth.''[10]

Coachbuilding flourished not only in the capital, which was the centre of the
horsy world in those days, but also in the provinces. There were, for example,
twenty-two coachbuilding firms in Northamptonshire and twenty-four in Oxford-
shire, according to the Post Office directory for 1877. In the whole country there
were about a thousand coachbuilding firms. Some of them were small concerns
initially. John Strangward, who was also the publican of the White Horse, Huntingdon, had a small firm, which made carts and wagons as well as carriages, and

77

The interior of a coach-wheelwright's shop at $4\frac{1}{2}$ Marshall Street, Soho in 1897.

employed only five people in 1861, according to the census taken in that year.[11] But by the end of the reign it had grown into a much bigger concern, making all kinds of carriages from four-in-hand coaches to pony carts, and with a good stock of vehicles always on display.

Some provincial coachbuilders gained more than a local reputation. Thomas R. Starey, of Lincoln Street and Lower Parliament Street, Nottingham, achieved an international reputation for his fine workmanship, winning one of the two first-class prize medals awarded to English coachbuilding firms at the Paris exhibition of 1855 and further awards at exhibitions in London, Oporto and Dublin. A framed set of his instructions for the care of carriages hung in the coach house or the harness room in many mews and stables throughout the country. The business, which had been started in 1786, had become one of the largest and most important firms in the city of Nottingham a century later.

In that age of unbridled opportunity for the enterprising businessman, fame and fortune were gained by many men who had the poorest start in life. Richard Andrews, known as Hampshire's Dick Whittington, who was mayor of Southampton for five successive years, started work as a farm boy at the age of eight or nine. A few years later he became apprenticed as a blacksmith to a stagecoach manufacturer and then, in 1832, at the age of thirty-three, he set up as a coachbuilder himself in a little back street of Southampton on his savings of £75. In the first year he made over £2,000 and within a dozen years he had built a new factory for £10,000 and was earning over £20,000 a year by selling 300 new and second-hand carriages.[12]

The biggest coachbuilding firms were to be found in London. In 1872, according to the Post Office directory, there were well over a hundred coachbuilding firms in the capital, many of them large concerns like N. and F. Thorn, coach and harness makers to the Queen, who never had less than 300 carriages in stock at their premises in Great Portland Street.[13] Hooper and Co. of Victoria Street, who also held the royal warrant, were one of the best coachbuilders. Other famous names were Holland's of Oxford Street; Robinson and Cook of Mount Street; Peters' of Park Street; and Morgan's of Long Acre.

Some carriages were exported to Europe, to the colonies and to that old standby of the English export trade, South America. Rich Parsee merchants and maharajahs – the Arabs of the Victorian world – made regular visits to England to buy horses, carriages and harness. One rich Indian prince had a harness which was so ornate that the horses were practically invisible: it was equipped with electric lights, which were switched on when he visited other palaces, so that he arrived in style, rather like Cinderella arriving at the ball.[14] But the very excellence of the English carriage restricted large export sales. "The trade," Philipson bemoaned, "is consequently falling chiefly into the hands of American manufacturers, who produce light, cheap vehicles, which, although lacking the solidity and the durability of English work, meet the wishes of the buyers in the matter of price."[15] Even by the Eighties, some American manufacturers using mass-production methods, standardized parts, and the cheap labour of young boys, were producing a buggy every ten minutes in their large factories.[16]

In general, English coachbuilders relied mainly on the domestic market. Although they did not run the same risks as horse dealers, some of them had the bare-faced impudence of copers when they came to make out their bills. A storage fee was charged for carriages awaiting collection after they had been repaired. Prices were usually quoted in guineas rather than in pounds, which added another 5%, and the ex-works price was usually some 10% higher than the quoted basic price. A light town chariot and harness which the Duke of Manchester ordered from Peters and Sons, the London coachbuilders, in 1856, cost 400 guineas; but extras, such as plating, ornaments, embossing and chasing crests, armorial bearings and covers added another £45 to the bill.[17]

People who wanted to trade in an old carriage, often found it just as difficult to obtain a fair price as we do for our motor-cars today. Even wealthy lords, who had been regular customers of the same coachbuilder for many years, found that these tradesmen could always produce good reasons for making the most paltry offers for their old vehicles, or for refusing to make any offer at all. This happened to the Earl of Radnor in 1842 when he decided to trade in two of his old carriages and to have a new town coach built. He wrote to his regular coachbuilder – L. Hopkinson of 77 High Holborn – and received the following letter in reply:

My Lord,
    In compliance with your Lordship's desire, I beg to inform you that the cost of a new Town Coach will vary from £450 to £550 dependent, of course, upon the style of finish. I built one last year which is much the sort I think would answer. It cost £450. Perhaps about £30 or £40 more would suffice to do all you require, but a full-dress Coach would exceed this by £100, or to any amount.
    If you desire to dispose of the two Carriages, the Travelling Coach and Chariot, I know of no mode but trying them a few weeks at the Pantechnicon and then per Auction. I, at once, must ask the favour to be excused purchasing or taking them in exchange. I am, and so we are all, so overstocked with second-hand carriages that they are quite useless. I was ashamed to allow you so low as £15 for your old Travelling Chariot. I have had it all this time at a cost of at least 15 more and wish anyone would give me £10 for it. Your Chariot is truly valuable where it is wanted, but I must lay out so much money upon it before it could be offered for sale, that it would not realize the expense of reparation.
    Your Coach is good and useful, but peculiar. Those who want such, will build. I

(Right above) *Elegance and splendour were combined in this superb equipage, which won first prize for action and pace at the Agricultural Hall Horse Show in 1872.*

(Right below) *The perfect proportions and curves of old-time carriages are finely delineated in this illustration from a trade journal.*

COACH BUILDERS. HARNESS MAKERS & SADDLERS ART JOURNAL

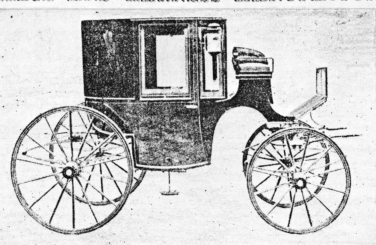

built one like it last year for Mr. Whitbread. Had yours been for sale, he would not have bought it. I have a Town Coach, second hand, which stands me in quite £300. It will not sell because it would cost £200 to make it as new. I should take £150 for it. I hope to be pardoned for entering into such particulars, but it is necessary I should state why I cannot take any more in exchange or purchase.

Your Lordship is, of course, the best judge, but I think you ought not to sell the Chariot. I would recommend to do a short repair at about one-third of the expense proposed and keep it for occasional use, and build a handsome new Town Chariot at £480, or not exceeding £500, and try to sell the Travelling Coach ...

A few days later, Hopkinson sent in his detailed estimate to "thoroughly repair, new paint and underspring" the chariot at a cost of £215 to £220; but as no order came, and his further pleas for "a personal conference" were ignored, he wrote again extolling the virtues of the £150 second-hand coach, which he had previously maintained would not sell at all and which, it now transpired, he had never previously seen!

I now wish very much that I could induce your Lordship to see the Coach I have offered to you. It was not in my sight when I wrote to you before and said I would take £150 for it. I will still say this and wish you to have it, but I have since had it brought into view and, as I expected, it is really worth double the money to any person who would be content with it, and use it as it is for three or four years. The colour is dark blue, picked Crimson, and the lining is Blue, with the Crimson lace and silk Cushions. This would not answer for you, therefore expense must be incurred, but for £350, or thereabouts, you may get into a most elegant, excellent carriage, which no one would for a Moment consider otherwise than new. And I will take on myself the responsibility of its proving nearly as good as any new one I can build. In short, I have now the opportunity to offer you a real bargain ...

Bargain or not, Hopkinson's offer was ignored, for by that time, quite justifiably, Lord Radnor had decided to employ a coachbuilder in the provinces where, on average, prices were 25% lower than in London. On the Earl of Sefton's recommendation he had his coach built by Mr. Gorst of 15 Great Charlotte Street, Liverpool, who could work to orders perfectly and "whose wheels and springs are

(Left) *Trade advertisements of 1892.*

966.—Coach making.

Carriages were made in spacious workshops by highly skilled craftsmen who often used quite simple tools.

quite unrivalled''. Another point in his favour was that he was willing to give the Earl of Radnor thirty guineas for his old chariot. When Hopkinson heard the news, he made one last indignant defence of his own skills, reputation and years of honest service:

I am quite aware you can get Carriages built for considerably less nominal sums than I can build *entirely new* for, but whether they will *wear as well as yours have done* is another thing entirely. You have had your Chariot above thirteen years; it has never failed once, and has cost very little in repairs. You had the Barouche above fifteen years and not quite new when you have had it first, though nearly so; it has worn equally well and will now bear reparation. I assure you, my Lord, that nothing but the best will do this, and no one *can charge less for such as I build* than I do. I can supply you with a new Coach for less, and it shall be worth the money, but it will not be entirely new (this, I will not disguise). The immense competition protects us all from extravagant profit in any trade. ...[18]

Coachbuilders, like other tradesmen, did have one genuine grievance in relation to some of their aristocratic customers, who often let their bills mount up not for weeks or months, but for many years. By 1865, the Duke of Manchester had accumulated over the years a debt of £1,150 with Peters, the London coachbuilder, a very considerable sum of money in those days. The duke always sent him a cheque for a few hundred pounds at decent intervals of six or seven years; but by 1869 the bill had reached a total of £1,448. Peters added a polite memorandum, in red ink, to his account:

> Would his Grace, the Duke of Manchester, be pleased to consider the subject of Interest upon the early part of the old bill! They having been of long standing – whilst the charges are only as usual. This matter is left for his Grace's consideration.

After a reasonable interval of a couple of years for reflection, the duke finally paid off most of the account, leaving a mere £118 unpaid as a foundation upon which to build in the next decade.[19]

In spite of the fine workmanship in carriages, their life was relatively brief, especially where smartness was the major consideration. Although a well-made carriage could last for a dozen years or more with occasional use and constant care, its normal life was only about five years. In addition to an annual service, a carriage usually needed repainting in the third or fourth year, and two years later the lining and the leatherwork usually had to be renewed at a total cost of perhaps £100. It was often cheaper in the long run to hire a carriage for a five-year period, as the coachmaker was responsible for all repairs, except those caused in accidents, and would repaint it once during the hiring period. A brougham of your own choice of colour and with your own crest on the panels, could be hired for £30 to £50 a year. Carriages could also be hired for much shorter periods, though this was much more expensive. In 1872, one London coachbuilder charged £5 for hiring a sociable landau for Ascot week.

Hire-purchase, which had been introduced by Richard Andrews of Southampton, "for the benefit of country gentlemen with incomes, but no ready money to spare", also became increasingly common in the Victorian age.[20] Payments were spread over a three-year and, later, a four-year period. Coachbuilders' advertisements commonly gave both the purchase and the hire-purchase price.

The Victoria became the most popular ladies' carriage, partly through the snob-appeal of its name.

Carriage bargains could be obtained at bazaars, pantechnicons and repositories where carriage brokers, the equivalent of copers in the horse-dealing world, always had some revamped carriage for sale "at a frightful sacrifice", more often of the purchaser's safety than of the broker's pocket. The paintwork was designed to survive nothing more inclement than exposure in the bazaar; the wheels were second-hand perquisites purchased from a coachman; the new lining concealed old, untreated patches of damp; and the crests on the panels had very often been added recently to give a fictitious warrant of its high-class origin. Two of the biggest carriage bazaars in London were situated in Belgravia and in Baker Street, where dozens of genuine, and more suspect, bargains could always be found, especially at the end of each season.

7

JOBMASTERS

Long before Queen Victoria's reign came to a close, the cost of foraging and stabling idle carriage horses, of endlessly repairing and replacing showy carriages, and of being cheated by lazy servants and dishonest tradesmen had become so immense that even some of the wealthiest aristocrats had started to use the services of a jobmaster. Some old ladies, too full of genteel pride to job their horses, might continue to drive behind their well-matched pair, whose blind eyes were fortunately on opposite sides of their heads so that they had one sound pair of eyes between them; but the English aristocracy has rarely allowed false pride to restrain its pragmatism. By the Nineties it was estimated that 80% of the sleek, well-groomed horses which hauled coaches to the Queen's drawing rooms and levees were on hire from jobmasters. Even the Queen herself had to go to Thomas Tilling of Peckham, the biggest jobmaster in the country, to hire twenty-five landaus, each with its pair of greys, for the use of foreign royalty during her jubilee celebrations in 1887.[1] And just before the First World War, the Earl of Derby had sixty horses on hire from Joshua East of Willesden. By the turn of the century there were 140 jobmasters in London and probably another 500 in the rest of the country.

Jobmasters could transform anyone into a king or a queen for the season, a month, or even the day, by supplying an expensive horse, a superlative carriage, and a coachman in top boots with a cockade in his hat. For longer hiring periods they would supply a crested carriage without too much genealogical investigation. The desire to ride in a carriage, even for a few hours, was so great that Dick Hunt, a jobmaster in Hove, Sussex, did a flourishing trade at the turn of the century by supplying residents and visitors with "a French-shaped victoria with rubber tyres, a coachman in breeches and boots, a horse worth £50 in the trade, brass-mounted harness and rosebuds in the bridle for ten shillings and six pence for two hours". He could also supply an equipage which was not "so smart" for seven shillings and

Thomas Tilling, the founder of the biggest and best-known firm of London jobmasters.

sixpence, though it was still guaranteed to excite the admiration and envy of the crowd far more than a common cab which cost only four shillings and sixpence for a two-hour drive along the promenade and through the town.[2]

Jobmasters flourished in Victorian and Edwardian times because they relieved customers of the heavy initial expense of purchasing horses, carriages and harness, and spread the risks and expenses of repairs and mishaps evenly among their numerous patrons. Through their specialized expertise and the maximum utilization of resources, jobmasters were able to keep their charges at about the same level as the expenses of a private owner. In the early Nineties, for example, it cost at least £200 a year to keep a brougham in London; but a jobmaster could supply a brougham, harness, a horse, forage, shoeing and a coachman, everything that was necessary except livery, for a total cost of about £210 a year. Any item could be hired separately: a carriage horse, including forage and shoeing, could be supplied for a hundred guineas a year and for twenty-four guineas a month during the season and for sixteen guineas during the rest of the year.

London jobmasters, who had some of the finest harness horses in the kingdom, preserved the quality of their stud by auctioning off up to one-third of it every year. Joshua East lost about twenty-five of his thousand carriage horses through illness every year, and sold off another 300 of the horses which were past their prime.[3]

86

Practically all of the jobmasters' carriage horses were geldings and most of them were greys. The finest and the most upstanding horses were reserved for work with a barouche.

Although jobmasters catered for a wide range of customers, doctors were among their steadiest clients. The Harley Street specialist, for reasons of status and prestige, needed a very different sort of horse from the humble, hard-working general practitioner. The consultant would job a pair of fine coach horses, which could travel fast and draw up in style at any stately door, impressing both his patient and, even more important, the neighbours, with his affluence and busyness; while the general practitioner, who had less chance of impressing neighbours as he was more often out at night than the consultant, needed a safe, reliable hackney, which would be happy to stand around in the rain for an hour and still be willing to haul his carriage safely back home again. Some specialists had as many as six horses on hire; but the general practitioner could usually afford only one, which he often rested on Sundays by making his rounds on foot.

Most of these horses were foraged by the jobmaster, but fed in the customer's own stables. Thomas Tilling's used to deliver the forage in their own carts once a week: four or five bushels of oats, a sack of chaff, one-and-a-half bushels of hay and two or three trusses of straw for each horse. Other jobmasters, like Robert Barley in the City, used to make a contract with a corn merchant such as Anstey's to forage their horses from a local branch.

To protect their valuable investments, all jobmasters put some restrictions on the horse's use. Journeys were restricted to a seven-mile radius from Charing Cross so that excessively long drives should not ruin the horse's fine action; and some jobmasters would not allow their horses to be used every day through fear that prolonged exposure to the elements would spoil their coats. Jobmasters' carriage horses all wore blinkers or "blinds" as much to protect their eyes from the ill-aimed lash of some badly-trained or drunken coachman as to prevent the horses from being frightened by the sight of the carriage bearing down on them from behind. (The horse has inherited its wide range of vision as a defensive mechanism from its wild state.) Some cautious jobmasters insisted that only their own coachmen should be employed, while others often gave the owner's coachman a gratuity to ensure that he treated the horses well. As a further precaution, some jobmasters sent their own veterinary surgeons round to their clients' mews and stables every week.

Some of the coachmen employed by jobmasters were casual workers who would line up at the entrance to the yard at 6 a.m. each day in search of work; but most of

The middle classes who could not afford a carriage of their own could always hire one – and a coachman or a groom – from a jobmaster.

them were regular employees who were paid a weekly wage of about thirty shillings and sometimes also received gratuities, or often abuse, from their society customers. Thomas Tilling boasted that "he would replace a lame horse, a broken carriage, or a drunken coachman within the hour", a process which had been greatly expedited by the introduction of a telephone service in the capital, with its eight initial subscribers, in 1879.[4] After some unfortunate coachman had been accused, falsely or not, of having had a glass of beer or a gill of rum instead of waiting soberly for his mistress in the cold night air, the butler would ring the jobmaster the next morning to demand a replacement. London jobmasters knew that it was useless to try to put a coachman with a tarnished reputation back on the society circuit without an interval of some months or even years; but if they thought that the coachman had been unjustly accused, or that his drunkenness was neither heinous nor habitual, they would find him employment in some other part of their business. Robert Barley would send them out with the millinery buses or the hatter's vans which, in Edwardian times, still travelled all over London delivering and displaying manufacturer's wares to shopkeepers.

Practically all jobmasters hired out horses to commercial firms as well as to the carriage trade, and many of them also owned cabs and buses and worked for the public sector. A small firm, like August's of Croydon, Surrey, which had sixty-six horses by the turn of the century, did a miscellaneous trade, sending some of their licensed cabs to Epsom every year to take rail travellers from the station up to the races; transporting wooden heels made by a local firm to a main line station in London for despatch to shoe factories in Northampton; and hiring out horses and a char-a-banc for workmen's excursions.[5] Bigger jobmasters had an even wider range of activities. Thomas Tilling, of Gloucester yeoman stock, had arrived in London in 1847 at the age of twenty-two with his grey mare, Kitty, and £30 to buy his first carriage, and by 1905, the firm owned 7,000 horses.[6] Tilling jobbed all over the country, from a heavy carthorse to a handy cob, supplying horses to "the duke, the doctor and the drayman".[7] He ran his own fleet of horse-drawn omnibuses and hansom cabs and supplied the fire brigade, the salvage corps and the police with horses from his main yard at Peckham, which was open day and night. Most big jobmasters had their own infirmaries and convalescent homes for horses; Tilling's infirmary, with sixty stalls and loose boxes, was about a quarter of a mile away from the headquarters. The stable roof was thatched inside to keep the temperature even. As their business expanded, jobmasters had to search for extra stabling and they took over many of the empty mews behind big houses and old stables in town and country inns.

In the course of their work, some jobmasters occasionally had unusual demands made upon their services. Dick Hunt recalls how a lady who was staying in Brighton asked him to provide her with a smart "turn-out" for a month. "I fitted her out with a smart cob and cart and she went for a trial drive, on her return expressed herself as very satisfied and asked me to call at the hotel that evening with the agreement. I sent up my card and was ushered up, where I was made very welcome with a cigar and a glass of wine. But the business in hand faded into the background at the lady's statement. She said: 'I may as well tell you what I want you here for. You are being watched, and my solicitor knows you are here and I want you to act as my co-respondent.'" Poor Hunt, baffled by this unexpected development, began unnecessarily, and rather ambiguously, to justify his presence by claiming an intimate knowledge not only of the hotel's proprietor but also of his wife. Much to his relief, the lady let him get away "without any complications".[8]

Funerals provided a profitable sideline for many jobmasters, as they were far more frequent at the turn of the century when the death rate was almost twice as high as it is today, and were conducted then with a lavish ostentation which is now reserved for heads of state. Even the very poorest people saved a penny or twopence a week in a burial club throughout their lives so that they could have the privilege of taking their first, and last, ride in a carriage when they were dead.

Funeral horses were mainly of the black, full-maned Flemish breed. Stallions were normally used, as geldings had a tendency to go brown with age. These horses were equally adept at trotting on long journeys or at bending their knees in an impressive way and flourishing their feet in a lugubrious slow march to the grave. Undertakers ensured that their clients went to their final resting place in good company as their horses were usually given uplifting names. The names in one stable included King John and Black Prince. Dottridge's, the biggest wholesale undertakers in the capital who also made coffins and repaired hearses, favoured more modern names such as General Booth, Huxley, Dr. Barnado, Dickens, Balfour, and Cardinal Manning. The horses were fitted out with black plumes and were often preceded by mutes, dressed in black, with long scarfs streaming from their black top hats, and carrying wands wreathed in crêpe. The hearse was also black, though later in the reign it became more fashionable to have a hearse with large glass panels, silver fittings and a purple hammercloth. Before the advent of the railways, a funeral procession could last for a week or more. When a lord died in London, his body was often taken back for burial in the family vault at his ancestral home in the countryside, which might be many miles away. Out of respect for the dead, the horses had to travel at a snail's pace through all the towns and villages *en route*, and could keep up a faster trot only in the open countryside.

Jobmasters were equally adept at providing a suitable equipage for more cheerful occasions and they reserved some of their most showy carriages and some of their finest greys for weddings. Tillings kept about forty horses specially for this purpose. But even though jobmasters could put on a magnificent show as far as horses, carriages and coachmen were concerned, they could never match the splendour of the reception accorded to a member of the private carriage-owning class, who could command the deferential respect of a whole segment of the countryside on such occasions. When Mr. James Edge and his bride arrived at Nottingham railway station on January 27, 1856, after their wedding celebrations, they were met by a barouche and pair, which he then drove himself to his ancestral home of Strelley Hall.

"At the boundary of the estate of Bilborough," an observer wrote, "marked out by a magnificent festoon of evergreens, pendant across the road from tree to tree of

(Right) *One of Tilling's horse-drawn buses – and its two-man crew.*

90

No great family occasion was ever complete without its carriage and perfectly attired coachman. It made one of the favourite subjects for Victorian photographers.

this beautifully wooded turnpike, the bridal *cortège* was met by about thirty mounted tenantry of the estates, each distinguished by wearing at the left breast a large white wedding favour in the form of a rosette, and all bearing white wands tipped with bunches of evergreens, festooned with white ribbons. The rest of the way, three miles in all, including the avenue of a mile in length, was one complete ovation. Preceded by a detachment, and followed by the main body of the mounted escort, the open carriage containing the party formed the nucleus of a gay procession, which was thenceforth cheered on its way with loud and earnest demonstrations of applause ...

"At the approach to the village of Bilborough, where a numerous party of villagers had drawn up to greet the lord and lady of the manor, a massive, magnificent triple arch was thrown across the turnpike, with a central inscription of 'Welcome' in gold letters on a blue ground; whilst the side arches were flanked by union jacks edged with golden-coloured net ... The most magnificent decorations of all, were at the principal entrance gate of the Strelley Avenue. Here a very splendidly embowered arch of evergreens, intermingled with flowers, was thrown up, streaming with flags, and surmounted by the inscription 'Health and Prosperity to Mr. and Mrs. Edge'.

"The *cortège* then entered the carriage drive, and amidst the shouts of considerable numbers assembled at the gate, at a more deliberate pace commenced the undulating ascent of the lovely grounds ... The bridegroom, having driven with a graceful sweep up to the door, the gallant escort formed in a semi-circle on the opposite verge of the drive, whilst the wives and daughters of the tenantry drew up in line on either side of the door. The bridal party looked uncommonly well, and seemed in the highest spirits at the hearty welcome thus accorded them.

"Mr. Edge, having handed out his bride, a perfect shower of bouquets was rained down at her feet, some of which she stooped and picked up, in acknowledgment of the compliment, whilst Mr. Edge himself adopted others. The signal being then given the crisp and frosty welkin was made to resound with three hearty cheers, led off by the cavaliers of the escort; and Mr. Edge, standing forward, said, 'My friends, I cannot help thanking you most sincerely for the hearty and flattering welcome you have given us. I am sure it is most gratifying to my feelings; and, as for decorations, they surprise me; I could not have believed that at this season of the year, the arches and arbours could have been so well and so handsomely got up.' Another hearty burst of acclamation followed this brief address; and the bride and bridegroom bowing to the assemblage entered their future abode of Strelley Hall."[9]

8

CABBIES AND CADS

For gig-less members of the middle classes who could not even afford the services of a jobmaster, there was no alternative means of urban transport until the underground railway and the bicycle were introduced later in the reign, other than walking, or using a cab, a horse-drawn omnibus or a tram. The Victorians walked a great deal more than we do today just as much through choice as necessity. When Viscount Palmerston became prime minister in his seventies, he "would trudge home on foot" from the House of Commons to Cambridge House in Piccadilly, often late at night or early in the morning, and write his official report of the debate for the Queen before he went to bed at 4 a.m. or 5 a.m., rising again only four or five hours later.[1] Other "middle-aged men, whose salaries have by no means increased in the same proportion as their families" walked to work every day through financial necessity. These clerks, the Pooters of the lower middle-class suburbs, would set out early in the morning from their homes in Camden Town, Islington and Pentonville to plod steadily towards their places of work in the City or the Inns of Court, passing the same people, whom they knew by sight, six days of the week; crossing the same streets at the same places at the same time as regularly as clockwork; and converging upon better-known acquaintances as they approached their places of employment but never stopping in that age of strict timekeeping to exchange anything but "a hurried salutation" even if they met a friend.[2] In 1860 over half-a-million people walked into the City every day, against some 170,000 who arrived in public and private vehicles.[3]

By the Sixties there were a few first-class rail commuters who lived right outside London, thirty miles or so away, and they were joined in the Seventies and the Eighties by more middle-ranking members of the middle classes.[4] But far more middle-class commuters lived in inner suburbs, travelling to work in horse-drawn omnibuses or less frequently in horse-drawn trams or hansom cabs.

94

THE OLD HACKNEY COACH.

The old hackney coach, 1886.

Although railways were quickly accepted by all classes in society as a suitable means of long-distance travel, horse-drawn public transport continued to bear a social stigma for most of the reign. Until the Eighties, no self-respecting lady would have ventured to make the indecent climb up the ladder to the top deck of an omnibus, while "grand ladies did not travel in omnibuses at all".[5] Horse-drawn trams, which were introduced in the 1860s, were generally thought to be even more socially inferior than omnibuses, even though there is some slight evidence that they may have been used initially in some cities, such as Leeds, by some members of the middle classes.[6] But, generally, trams were despised. Dick Hunt, the Hove jobmaster, firmly believed that their introduction marked the beginning of the end of Brighton as a fashionable resort. "Up to that date," he wrote, "the season of prosperity in Brighton was from October to January. The wealthy classes brought down their horses, carriages and servants, filled the hotels, rented mansions and spent money. When they came and saw the trams commandeering the roads, they ceased to visit Brighton."[7]

Even cabs had an unsavoury reputation, which was not entirely unmerited, so that for many years it was considered quite immodest for a lady to ride in one alone. The hansom cab's predecessor, the hackney coach, had acquired a really shameful reputation in the early years of the nineteenth century, when Regency bucks started to hire them for their night-time sports. One old hackney coachman recalled in the Sixties how he used to drive Lord Barrymore on his rounds of the London brothels two or three nights a week. "After waiting till near daylight, or till daylight, I've carried my lord, girls and all – fine, dressed-up madams – to Billingsgate, and there I've left them to breakfast at some queer place, or to slang with fishwives. What times them was, to be sure!

"One night I drove Lord Barrymore to Mother Cummins's in Lisle Street, and when she saw who it was, she swore out of the window, that she wouldn't let him in – he and some such rackety fellows had broken so many things the last time they were there, and had disgraced her, as she called it, to the neighbourhood."

Lord Barrymore, who had invented the tiger and had fallen into the habit of calling all drivers by that name, was not to be resisted by any madam, and said: "Knock at the door, tiger, and knock till they answer it." The driver did so repeatedly until every drop of water in the house had been emptied over them; but Mother Cummins remained adamant and Lord Barrymore, for once, had to admit defeat and go off home.[8] But he had his own anti-social methods of relieving his frustrations. Sometimes, while he was driving home to Wargrave, Berkshire, in his high-built phaeton late at night, he would lash out at the darkened windows of village houses – "fanning the daylights", as he called it – and roar with laughter as he left behind a tinkling trail of shattered glass.[9]

A few old decrepit hackney coaches survived into the early years of Victoria's long reign, some of them painted "a dingy yellow colour (like a bilious brunette)", as Dickens wrote in *Sketches by Boz*.[10] One Victorian lord remembered that "the old hackney coach was usually a broken-down, rickety vehicle, that had evidently seen

(Right above) *A hansom cab, the predecessor of the London taxi.*

(Right below) *A horse bus at the Royal Huts Hotel, Hindhead, Surrey in 1905.*

96

EASTERN & CHATHAM RAILWAY.
S ROUTES TO THE CONTINENT
STEND FOLKESTONE & BOULOGNE, QUEENBOROUGH & FLUSHING   CRYSTAL PALACE

BOOK HERE FOR CRYSTAL PALACE
GREAT WESTERN RAILWAY
TRAINS FROM AND TO THIS STATION

Victoria Station, London

better days; it usually bore the arms and crest of some noble family; the lining, torn and faded, showed signs of former grandeur, as did the harness, now patched and tied together with string. The horses looked more fit to furnish a meal for a pack of hungry fox-hounds than to go through their daily work."[11]

Something much smarter than an aristocrat's discarded coach was demanded by the status-conscious middle classes for whom outward appearance was of such immense importance, and to meet their needs, new types of cabs were introduced including a curious two-wheeled cabriolet, with the driver perched on a little seat beside the passengers, known as a "coffin cab" because of the shape of the hood; and the Bulnois cab with a door at the rear which proved too big a temptation for bilkers. Other kinds of cabs were introduced later, including one with three wheels, but the only cabs which survived throughout Victorian and Edwardian times were the four-wheeled clarence and the two-wheeled hansom.

The clarence, which was more familiarly known as the "growler" owing to the deafening noise it made particularly on stone or macadam roads, became the cab-of-all-work, equally suitable for parties of soldiers and sailors returning home on leave, servant girls moving their boxes to a new situation in some distant suburb, working-class wedding parties, patients going to hospital, and nervous old ladies who were too genteel to use a more dashing hansom cab. In time, many of these clarences became as decrepit as the old hackney coaches, with their loose, rattling windows adding a tremulous note to the growling bass line; scratched varnish, peeling paint and dirty straw littering the floor; and surly coachmen, who were as ancient and overworked as their horses, with a shabby old horse-cloth thrown over their knees to bring some warmth back into their rheumatic limbs.

In contrast, the average hansom cab was a much smarter affair. The original hansom cab, designed by an architect of that name in 1834, was like a huge packing case, with a slightly sloping roof, suspended between two enormous wheels which were seven feet six inches in diameter; but the cab which became such a familiar feature of Victorian streets was a very different looking vehicle. It was designed by John Chapman two years later, but because he sold the patent to the Hansom Cab Company, his vehicle still bears the name of a rival designer. The

(Left above) *A design drawing for a hansom cab, c. 1898.*

(Left below) *The forecourt outside Victoria Station crowded with hansom cabs in 1909.*

driver sat at the back, controlling the distant horse by long reins which stretched over the roof, opening the padded leather flap doors which gave access to the passenger seats by means of a lever and chains, and communicating with the passengers through a small trapdoor in the roof. The hansom cab was not particularly easy to drive as the cabbie could see only the top of the horse's head and scarcely anything of the wheels, but the high seat, and years of experience, had made most of them fast, skilful drivers, who were able to spot a gap from a great distance and judge it to an inch, and to keep their horse on its feet even on the most slippery surface.

You had to be something of an athlete to get into a hansom cab, which was an additional reason for its not being favoured by old ladies or stout parties. First, you had to put one foot on a small iron step about eighteen inches off the ground and then, with a graceful pirouette, lodge your other foot on the platform up above. In executing this gymnastic turn, many ladies had their hats knocked off by the overhanging reins or soiled their precious gowns on the rim of the nearby wheel. The hansom cab's main virtue was its snug privacy. There was just enough room for a couple to snuggle up beside each other on the padded leather seat and the window blinds could be lowered to ensure anonymity. Some of the smartest cabs were owned by the twentieth Earl of Shrewsbury and Talbot, who was the first cab proprietor to replace the old iron-hooped wheels with solid rubber tyres in the Eighties.

London cabbies were a special breed of men, independent, proud, quick-witted, disputatious, who were almost permanently engaged in a long war of attrition with proprietors, parliament, the police, railway companies and the middle classes who were their main customers. Most of them were London-born, with a wide general knowledge acquired through hours of newspaper reading and long discussion while they were waiting for a fare, and with an inherited gift of Cockney wit and repartee. One cabby, who was known as "Palace Yard Jack" because he was a favourite among M.P.s, was given a sovereign in mistake for a shilling when he drove Lord John Russell home one night. The next night, Russell challenged him and "Palace Yard Jack" admitted that he had bought a pair of boots with the sovereign, even though he realized that Russell had made a mistake. "Look, my lord," he said, displaying them for inspection, "they're Russells, not Wellingtons", and Lord John walked away smiling.[12] Anecdotes such as this, and other

(Right) *Hansom cabs were sometimes as difficult to find at night as taxis are in present times.*

scraps of recondite information imparted by knowledgeable passengers, circulated quickly through the ranks, adding to the knowledge and amusement of the cabbies.

A small number of cabbies, who usually had the smartest turn-outs, were owner-drivers, but the majority hired their horses and cabs by the day or the night from small proprietors owning from two to five hansoms. The cabby had to pay up to twenty-five shillings a day in the season and up to fifteen shillings at other times of the year to hire the cab. He also had to provide his own oil for the lamps, decorative flowers and bells for the horse, and sometimes a mat for the passenger compartment. In addition, he had to give the horsekeeper in the proprietor's yard a threepenny tip if he wanted to get a well-groomed, good-looking, or "gassy" horse as he called it and not some broken-down old screw, and a similar amount to the washer who cleaned the outside of the cab, for they, no less than he, depended on tips and perquisites to supplement their incomes in that low-wage era. Every time the cabby went to a cab stand to get a drink of water for his horse and something stronger for himself, he had to pay the waterman a penny and another halfpenny if it was hired while it was there.

The hiring system, with its extortionate charges was the basic cause of most of the cabby's troubles, making him resentful of avaricious proprietors, antagonistic towards parliament which controlled the fares, and scathingly contemptuous of tight-fisted customers who gave him the exact fare, sometimes carefully counted out in halfpennies and farthings. One well-dressed cabby, who was known as the "King of the Cabmen" treated his clients with such high disdain that his colleagues falsely credited him with aristocratic origins though he had previously been a tailor by trade: any customer who had the temerity to offer only the legal fare was likely to be asked scornfully if he would like to toss for it, double or quits. The "King" had an equal lack of respect for authority. When the police refused to let him park his cab outside his favourite coffee shop, he started to dine in the West End instead, spreading a snow-white table cloth on the top of his cab from which he sometimes ate a splendid dinner sent out by sympathetic members of a nearby gentleman's club.[13]

Although the middle classes believed in free enterprise and uncontrolled profits for themselves, they were unwilling to let cabbies share in their philosophy and succeeded in persuading the reformed parliament to reduce cab fares. London cabbies had participated in the extravagant enthusiasm for the Great Exhibition of 1851 by a great magnification of their fares for the six million ignorant foreign and provincial visitors. It became even more difficult for a Londoner, who knew the

Aunt Virginia. "Good Gracious, Girls, I declare I'm quite Afraid to Get Out! Look at the Cabman! He's got Mistletoe in his Hat!!"

Cabbies were one of the main targets of Punch'*s humour for many years.*

proper rates, to hire a cab, until the police stepped in. Up to that time, London "bobbies" still retained some of their initial unpopularity among the middle classes as intruders upon the liberties of free-born Englishmen; but their prosecutions of cabmen helped to create a new image of the kind, helpful policeman. *Punch*, which was then far more concerned with comfort at home than imperialist adventures abroad, proclaimed that the police had started to gain the warm place in the "affections of the people" that had once been reserved for soldiers and sailors. "The taking of a foreign fort seems to sink into insignificance before the taking of a refractory cabman's number – for the simple reason that we do not want and do not care for foreign forts; but our comfort very much depends on the good behaviour of our native cabmen."[14] Two years later, parliament reduced cab fares in central London from eightpence to sixpence a mile which led to a short-lived strike among cabmen. Although the minimum fare was later raised to a shilling for two miles, the battle over fares – and tips – went on for many more years.

In the Seventies, a new champion of the cab-using public arose in the formidable form of Mrs. Caroline Giacometti Prodgers who, in spite of her marriage to an

A cab stand with growlers and hansom cabs in 1888.

Austrian naval captain, had lost none of her British pluck. She was readmitted to British nationality in 1875 after her divorce. Her mere appearance at her front door was sufficient to empty the cab stands and to clear the neighbouring streets of all hansoms and growlers as their cabbies drove off furiously with loathing in their hearts. Mrs. Prodgers had acquired such a detailed knowledge of the capital's topography that she could calculate a two-mile journey to the foot, when she would alight and tender the exact fare. Summonses and counter-summonses crackled off like cross fire between Mrs. Prodgers and the cabbies, but she invariably won. She became such an object of loathing among cabbies that they even burnt her effigy on Guy Fawkes night in 1876 and could still be heard indignantly discussing her "misdeeds" after her death in 1890.

Although the middle classes wanted to step into a cab directly they wanted one, none of them desired cabs, with their red-nosed, pot-bellied drivers to be stationed outside their own front doors day and night. As a result, cab stands were banished to the middle of the streets, as many still are, or situated in out-of-the-way places or by blank walls. Through the opposition of householders and shopkeepers, there were far fewer cab stands in central London than were needed, so that cabmen were forced to "crawl" along the streets in search of fares, adding considerably to the traffic congestion, a practice which has persisted with indomitable English conservatism to the present day. Cabbies, not unnaturally, became highly indignant when they were prosecuted by the police for crawling, as there was often no alternative but to go off to other streets, miles away, where they might be unable to find a fare. Mr. Samuel Michaels, the president of the London Cab Drivers' Union, told an inquiry in 1905: "What I want to point out is, the cab that is called a crawling cab is usually not a crawling cab at all. For instance, we find in the Strand all day long, perhaps a hundred cabs per hour setting down fares. Those cabs may have come five or six miles, and the result is, when the horse gets there, it is tired, and as there is insufficient ranking accommodation, although the men would be prepared to put up on the rank in the Strand, unfortunately that rank is full. No one would suggest that having come five or six miles, a man is to take his whip out of the socket, and slash his horse anywhere or everywhere."[15]

Another grievance arose from the "privileged cab" system under which only those cabbies who paid a fee of from two to five shillings a week were allowed to wait for fares at railway stations. As a consequence, it was usually far more difficult to get a cab at one of the London rail termini than it is today and there was even greater congestion at the entrances. Mr. Lawrence Russell, who had been a cab driver for fifteen years, told the same inquiry: "Under the present system (and this applies to nearly all the stations except Waterloo and Vauxhall), after setting down a fare, they can go in whatever direction they like, except on to the premises of the railway company, and you will find hundreds of those empty cabs meeting hundreds of other railway cabs going in opposite directions."[16]

The cabby's lot was not a happy one. To make sufficient money to pay the hiring fee, a man might have to drive up to fifty miles a day before he could pocket any of the fares himself. Some cabbies, known in the trade as long-day men, had to start work at nine or ten in the morning, go back to the yard in the afternoon to change the horse, and continue working until the small hours of the morning, when they finally returned to the yard, sometimes almost falling off their seat through exhaustion or drink, or more often both, into the arms of their patient, waiting wife. For part of the night, they would hand over the reins to a "buck", an unlicensed driver or cabby who had lost his licence through some misdemeanour. These "bucks" were generally "confirmed sots" of "no fixed abode", who dozed in tap rooms during the day and slept in cabs at night, making a few pence a day by "rubbing up" the panels, windows and brass fittings of the cabs, driving at night and taking half the proceeds, and robbing any passenger whom they found drunk or asleep in the cab.[17]

The long-day system was responsible for much of the cruelty to cab horses as both the horses and their drivers became irritable, stubborn and exhausted by the early hours of the morning. Victorian newspapers were full of reports of cruelty to cab horses. William Thomas, a long-day man employed by Richard Casey a cab proprietor of Grays Inn Road, was fined forty shillings, or fourteen days' imprisonment, after he had brought his horse back to the yard at 3 a.m. "scored with weals" and with one of its shoes missing and the hoof broken.[18] Another cabman, William Harford, who worked for Mr. W. Newton of Little Queen Street, Westminster, was sentenced to two months' hard labour for unmercifully whipping his horse until it was "one mass of congealed blood and wounds" from its haunch, down one of its thighs to the fetlock. The whip had a firm thick knot at the end, what cabmen called a "button".[19]

The Royal Society for the Prevention of Cruelty to Animals had mercy patrols which visited the London cab stands. In 1856 it was reported that "the monthly returns of the Society's operations show that frequently as many as a dozen horses working in cabs, are allowed by their owners to be destroyed in the presence of the Society's constables in order to avoid prosecutions".[20] Most cab horses did not have a very long working life. Mr. William Sheather, one of the large London cab proprietors with a hundred horses, said that their useful life varied considerably from ten months to ten years; but the average was estimated by another expert at less than two years.[21] There was some improvement in conditions for both cabbies and horses when the Home Secretary intervened to fix fairer daily hiring charges, after a strike by London cabmen from May 15 to June 11, 1894.[22]

By the turn of the century there were 3,600 cab proprietors in the capital, including a surprisingly large number of women, some of whom, like the good-looking but universally detested "Queen of Hell" were no less grasping than male proprietors. Outside London, cabmen were usually paid a weekly wage though this was often miserably low. Accounts kept by Mr. J. M. Walker, a Leeds cab proprietor, show that his drivers received from eighteen shillings to £1 a week in 1891, the same wage as his horsekeepers.[23]

For those members of the middle classes who could not afford to hire a cab, the horse-drawn omnibus provided a cheap alternative form of urban transport. They were used mainly by suburban commuters, lady-shoppers, and people travelling to and from railway stations. The omnibus originated in France and for many years there was a strong French connection. The first regular service in London from Paddington to the Bank was started on July 4, 1829, by George Shillibeer, an

Cab drivers having a meal break on the Embankment.

English coachbuilder who had been working in Paris. The fare was one shilling, with the free use of the magazines and newspapers which were provided. In 1856, the London General Omnibus Company, which was a French concern in spite of its name, started operations in London with fifty omnibuses and 500 horses; by the Nineties it had become the biggest omnibus company in the world with 10,000 horses and 1,000 buses which travelled a total distance of 20,000 miles a year. There were many other companies in the capital including the London Road Car Company with about 3,000 horses, which was the second largest concern; the Metropolitan Railway Omnibus Company, whose vehicles had six first-class seats up in front concealed behind a curtain; and some one-bus firms. In the provinces, omnibuses were often run by cab proprietors.

The London omnibuses were colour-coded so that everyone knew, for example, that the Atlas light green was bound for the West End and the dark green for the City; but both these colours and even the firms' names were also used by the many unlicensed "pirate" omnibuses, which operated illegally from Shillibeer's time right up to the Edwardian age. These pirate buses preyed on innocent women and ignorant foreigners by charging extortionate fares; terminating their journeys long before the suburban destination had been reached; and giving short change to passengers. They usually carried one or two hired "toughs" to threaten any passenger who dared to protest and, sometimes, a pickpocket who worked in collusion with the driver and the conductor. Some employed a couple of fashionably-dressed ladies, who perched like elegant decoys on the outside seats to lure unsuspecting victims to what seemed to be a respectable vehicle. The pirates' favourite spot was Oxford Street with its crowds of lady-shoppers; but they were also to be found in all parts of London, crawling along the streets in search of victims. The licensed proprietors combined to fight the pirates by instructing their own drivers to follow any pirate until it left the streets, which led to some interminable journeys for passengers in both vehicles as the pirate sought to evade its "nurse". The crews were not always as antagonistic towards each other as the proprietors. One indignant owner once found a pirate and a licensed omnibus parked empty outside an inn, while inside the two crews were happily engaged in drinking beer and playing a quiet game of skittles![24]

The horse-drawn omnibus was neither a particularly speedy nor a comfortable vehicle, travelling on average at about 5 m.p.h. and providing cramped accommodation. Although most omnibuses were licensed to carry only ten to twelve passengers inside and another ten to fourteen outside, most conductors, who pocketed many of the fares themselves until the Nineties, were always willing to admit an extra passenger or two in spite of the discomfort it caused to other passengers. The buses were hot and stuffy inside and darkened by the wooden advertisement boards which blocked out much of the light from the side windows. In winter, the floor was littered with straw. By law, each passenger was entitled to sixteen inches of seat space; but this was often considerably reduced by the presence of selfish and cantankerous stout parties who spread out their legs to relieve the pressure on their paunch, so that some passengers carried a tape measure with them to ensure that they got their legal ration of space! On the open upper deck, passengers sat on back-to-back seats in the knifeboard omnibus which had been introduced in 1850 and on more comfortable, forward-facing seats in the garden-seat omnibus which was introduced thirty years later. "It was not until garden seats and roomy staircases took the place of the ladder and knifeboard back-to-back seats and skirts became more manageable," wrote Mrs. Peel, "that women ventured to the top of the omnibus."[25] This female departure caused many raised male eyes and problems of etiquette, though the omnipresent, omniscient "Madge" of *Truth* soon set everything to rights. "There seems to be an idea in the lowly classes," she wrote, "that it is correct to precede a lady in ascending steps or

A street scene in Piccadilly by the Burlington Arcade when the horse still ruled.

stairs. This is not in accordance with the practice of good society. If circumstances do not admit of the two walking abreast, the lady goes first."[26]

The most coveted place in the omnibus was on the seat beside the driver, just as it had been in the old coaching days when young aristocrats had acquired their first hints about the mystery of four-in-hand driving by travelling on the coachman's box. Every morning, City gents who had never got over their infantile notions of becoming a bus driver, would grasp the leather strap let down by the driver and clamber up the front wheel to the seat above.[27] They often had an adventurous journey to work, particularly on those routes where rival companies were engaged in what *Punch* called "the fine old English sport of racing". The buses sped along on opposite sides of a cab stand in the middle of the road, sometimes colliding and nearly overturning as they converged at the end of the rank. They

The Waterside entrance to Cremorne Gardens, with hansom cab.

careered wildly from one side of the street to the other to pick up passengers as they were not obliged to stop as near as possible to the left-hand side of the road until 1867.[28]

The drivers, who were paid a basic wage of six shillings for a twelve-hour day, were of mixed origins including butchers, builders, farmers, horsebreakers, cheesemongers, old stagecoachmen, broken-down gentlemen, turfmen, servants, grooms and mechanics. Their main problem then, as it is for bus drivers today, was trying to keep on schedule in the congested streets. One driver, a former builder, who had been on the buses for fourteen years, told Mayhew in 1861: "I must keep exact time at every place where a time-keeper's stationed. Not a minute's excused – there's a fine for the least delay . . . If I've been blocked, I must make up for the block by galloping; and if I'm seen to gallop, and anybody tells our people, I'm called over the coals."[29]

Bus drivers had inherited some of the stagecoachman's romantic appeal, but the rude and avaricious conductors had been almost universally detested from the start and were soon known colloquially as cads. *Punch*, that sturdy champion of the metropolitan middle classes, conducted a long campaign against those cads who always quoted a fare of twopence or threepence at the start of a journey which had invariably been inflated to sixpence at the end.[30] Conductors received nominal wages of four to five shillings a day, but by cheating both the customers and the company they made up to an extra £5 or £6 a week, which they shared with the driver. It was easy for them to pocket fares, as tickets were not issued on the majority of buses. Companies employed private detectives or "spots", who travelled on the buses to ensure that the conductor's takings corresponded with the number of passengers, but only a minority of dishonest conductors were ever caught, and even if they were, there were always equally dishonest cads to take their place. It was not until the heavy snowstorms of 1891 reduced the volume of traffic and the profits of the omnibus companies, that the biggest concern, the London General Omnibus Company, decided to introduce tickets. In defence of their illegitimate private enterprise, all London busmen stopped work; but the strike, in spite of helpful contributions to the strike fund by pirate concerns, lasted only a week.[31]

Omnibuses which set out from railway stations attracted another kind of free-booter: bare-footed street urchins who would run along beside the bus for up to four or five miles in the hope of acting as a porter when passengers reached their destination. "Them poor young 'uns," said one bus driver, "is arnin what I calls a reg'lar hard penny. They are a-lookin' out arter the luggage; and because they runs it down all the way from the railway, they thinks they got a right to the porterage."[32]

The omnibus companies were among the biggest consumers of horses in the capital. The horses, which were practically all mares, were engaged in their heavy arduous work for an average period of four-and-a-half years before they were sold to a knacker for £5 apiece.[33] The biggest knacker in London was Harrison, Barber and Co., whose main depot was in Garratt Lane, Wandsworth, where 26,000 horses underwent the same process of "slaying and flaying, boning and boiling" every year. The horses' eyes were covered with a shade before they were beheaded with an axe in a spacious kitchen with polished coppers and boilers stretching the whole length of two of the walls. Not a bone, not an ounce of flesh, not a strip of hide was wasted in this grisly business, the other side of Victorian transport, which

With all the manure on city streets, shoeblacks did a roaring trade.

would have sickened proud carriage owners and respectable omnibus passengers if they had ever visited these vast extermination camps. The horseshoes were ripped off and sold to farriers. The flesh was flayed with knives and hooked on to a beam before the hide was peeled off in the longest possible strips. The bones were sold to make artificial fertilizers and buttons. The hooves were boiled for glue. The tails and manes were sold to upholsterers and were also used for making fishing lines.[34] The flesh was boiled and sold to East End butchers who "made up a pound of meat in six ha'porths" and displayed it in their windows on skewers.[35] The hides were the most valuable item with many different uses from making weather-proof linings for carriages to leather guards for cavalry breeches. And – the final indignity – some of the hide was also used for making whip thongs to control the next generation of horses.

9

PERILS OF THE ROADS

The Victorians never succceded in coping with the problems of urban transport. Achievement stopped short at the railway stations. In the streets outside, the traffic jams grew to uncontrollable proportions, the towns and cities became increasingly polluted, and the toll of accidents among horses, passengers and pedestrians continued to mount.

The railways had brought about a great deterioration in the main highways, but for many years there was no compensatory improvement in urban roads. In 1850, *Punch* compared the streets of London with the surface of the moon, newly discovered by telescopic observation to consist of an alternation of lofty eminences and profound chasms. Nearly forty years later, there had been little improvement with the road between Northumberland Avenue and St. Stephen's Club on the Embankment "one mass of depressions" which caused the wheels of carriages to "fly about in all directions"; the paving stones at Charing Cross sinking one below the other "creating great pools of water like stagnant lakes"; and streets in many places "swimming with mud".[1]

The many boards and vestries which administered the roads were no less tyrannical than the bureaucrats of today in deciding what kind of road surface the rate-paying public should have to endure. Until the Seventies, there were three main kinds of urban road, all of which had different defects. Some roads were paved with huge granite blocks or setts, usually transported from Aberdeen by sea, which provided a reasonably firm surface for heavy traffic until they began to wear or to subside. But they gave off great clouds of choking dust after a few years' use; they were slippery for horses in dry weather; and their worst feature was the reverberating noise they produced which was almost as deafening as that given off by older cobblestones. In the Sixties about three-quarters of the capital's roads were macadamized. The surface consisted of little stones, no more than an inch in any of their dimensions, which, in theory, should have been compacted into a firm surface by the wheels of carriages and other vehicles. Although they were less noisy than granite setts and much cheaper to construct, macadamized roads had many loose stones on the surface which were a danger to horses and pedestrians alike and they were dusty in dry weather and extremely muddy in wet. The newest form of road surface, introduced at about the time of the Great Exhibition, was constructed of wooden blocks. They were much quieter than any other kind of road, having first been used in London outside the Old Bailey so that judges could hear themselves speak; but they were expensive to build and slippery when damp.

London trailed far behind Paris and many English provincial cities in the construction of better roads. The French had been building smooth, asphalt roads, which were free from mud, from the 1830s and using steam rollers experimentally since 1859, at a time when London contractors were still being allowed to "throw down angular blocks of hard stone upon the road to a depth of several inches without binding them together".[2] "What fools the French must think us," bemoaned the patriotic Mr. Punch, "when they see us strewing lumps of granite loosely in our roadways, and wearing out our carriage-wheels in grinding it to slush."[3] It took the combined force of the aristocracy, the Royal Society for the Prevention of Cruelty to Animals and *Punch* to propel the bureaucratic vestries into action. Lord Rothschild let it be known that he was going to sue the local road surveyor for damage to his valuable carriage horses; the RSPCA asked carriage-owners to provide evidence of injury to horses so that it could launch a prosecution; while *Punch* maintained its mordant attacks.[4] The cities of Liverpool, Leeds and Birmingham had all started to use steam rollers before London's authorities eventually decided to give them a trial. "Fancy London without mud," *Punch* enthused in 1868. "What a blessing to look forward to!"[5]

There was no total improvement in roads, however, until motor-cars made tar and bitumen surfaces essential as their fast-spinning pneumatic tyres sucked up the dust from macadam roads in such dense clouds that people could scarcely breathe. The Victorians continued to live with their pollution. The rumbling reverberations of carriage wheels on granite setts was so loud that straw had to be

(Right) *Fallen and dying horses were a familiar sight in city centres. This illustration appeared in* The Animal World *published by the Royal Society for the Prevention of Cruelty to Animals.*

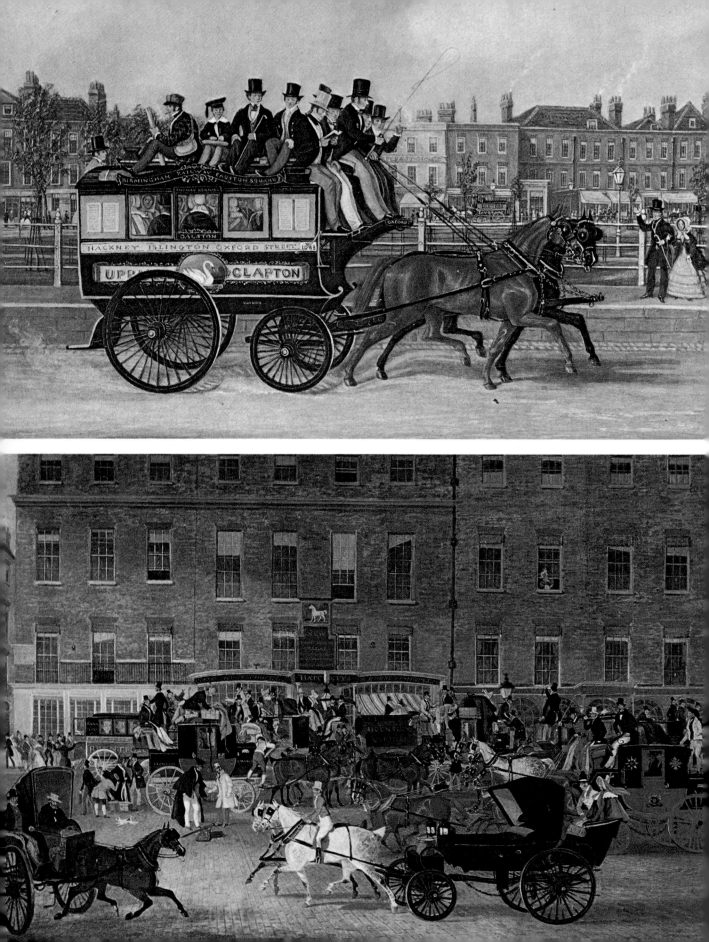

strewn outside hospitals and the houses of the sick and dying to lessen the din. The Marquis of Hertford never lived in his town house in Piccadilly again after the local vestry had refused to replace the granite setts on the road outside with quieter macadam.[6] The dust was so dense in some areas of London, such as Regent's Park, that windows were never opened on windy days. One tradesman who had supplied a gentleman with the same silk damask curtains for his town and country residences found that they lasted almost twice as long in the country because they were not damaged by dust.[7] In rain, or when the macadamized roads were watered to lay the dust, the roads became a sea of mud. Contrary to some popular belief, the late Victorian middle classes were not always optimistic, smug and satisfied with their lot. Comparing the ancient Carthaginians with nineteenth-century Londoners, (which was quite a stretch of the imagination), Athol Maudslay wrote in 1888: "What we have lost in ignorance and barbarism, we have gained in a highly-cultivated system of perpetual dirt in wet weather, and dust in dry weather ... Dust rising from the street injures the interior of our houses; whereas mud is destructive to one's carriages, clothes and boots."[8]

Mud and dust were not the only things which made the streets of all big towns and cities filthy. Every day a horse excretes on average something like 45 lb. of dung. In aggregate, this vast accumulation of horse droppings created an enormous scavenging problem which the Victorians never solved, and a great health hazard. Sir Henry Thompson, the eminent English surgeon, wrote: "The air in towns is ... in dry weather loaded with dust, a great part of which is composed of dried and pulverized horse manure. In wet weather, fluid manure from the same source is absorbed by, and then exhaled from, the road or wood pavement with similarly injurious effects."[9] In the 1830s, it has been estimated, English towns had to dispose of some 3,000,000 tons of horse droppings every year, which had more than trebled to 10,000,000 tons by the end of the century.[10]

Local authorities used many different methods in their vain efforts to bring some semblance of cleanliness to urban streets. Vestries and boards of works in London used 1,500 horses to remove 1,300,000 cart-loads of refuse from the streets every year, and there were another 600 horses on contract from McNamara's of Fins-

(Left above) *Kendall's Omnibus at Islington Green – a painting by James Pollard, 1848.*

(Left below) *Hatchetts – The White Horse Cellar, Piccadilly – a painting by James Pollard.*

VESTED INTERESTS.

Sweeper. "IF YOU DON'T GET OFF MY CROSSIN', I'LL 'EV YOUR NUMBER!"

A Punch *cartoon of the 1850s showed a fitting sense of propriety.*

bury.[11] In the Eighties, the City of London had to dispose every year of 30,000 tons of wet "slop" and street sweepings which consisted largely of "horse droppings, and the remainder of hay, straw, fragments of packing materials and the waste of all sorts produced by an enormous traffic": it was taken to Lett's Wharf on the southern bank of the Thames near Waterloo Bridge and transported by barge to farmers and market gardeners.[12] In Leeds, the slush and scrapings from macadamized roads were piled up beside the road or carted to dumps on the outskirts of the city to be used later in road-making; while the wet slop was taken to depots and sold to farmers at one shilling and sixpence per cubic yard.[13]

Some London boroughs employed paupers at wages of from ten to twelve shillings a week to sweep the streets. In 1855, both Chelsea and St. Marylebone employed on average seventy-two paupers in this way.[14] The eminent engineer, Joseph Whitworth (later Sir Joseph) invented a horse-drawn mechanical sweeper which was first tried out in Manchester on February 13, 1844.[15] But many streets in all parts of the country continued to be swept by hand for many years after that. Every fashionable square, every main street, every large bank had its own free-lance crossing sweeper, who made a few pence a day by sweeping a clear passage for ladies and gentlemen, opening carriage doors, and occasionally running errands or delivering parcels. One of the best-known London crossing sweepers in the Sixties was Billy, an old, white-haired man with "a face as red as a love apple, and cheeks streaked with little veins," who operated in Cavendish Square. In 1861 he told Mayhew that he could remember much better times, thirty years before, when crossing sweeping was a proud and prosperous profession. His hat was always full of money at Christmas and the Duke of Portland used to give him seven shillings and sixpence regularly every week; but times had changed, and crossing sweepers were lucky to make a shilling a day.[16] Neither these free-lance efforts nor the authorities' activities could keep back the sea of mud which seeped and oozed out of so many streets. The long, trailing skirts of society ladies soon became smeared with a mixture of mud and dung if they ventured to set a dainty foot in the road: it was the unenviable task of the first footmen to scrape and brush the dirt and manure from the bottom hem of his mistress's long frocks.

The weather had a much greater effect on urban traffic than it does today. A sudden shower brought horses to their knees or to the ground by their dozen. William Haywood, the Surveyor to the Commissioners of Sewers in the City of London, conducted a survey on fifty working days in 1872 and found that, on average, a horse could travel only 191 miles on asphalt, 132 miles on granite setts, and 330 miles on wooden blocks before it fell.[17] Even if the horse was seriously injured, it had to lie sprawling in agony on the ground until the master or his veterinary surgeon arrived, as a mere coachman had no authority to order the destruction of one of his master's valuable carriage horses. A protesting crowd always gathered at such incidents and there were many indignant letters in the Press about the unnecessary suffering to horses. Ice and snow always resulted in a large crop of serious accidents, even though the horses' shoes were rough nailed and soft soap was applied to prevent the snow from balling; and there were many calls on the services of the horse ambulances which were used to remove dead or maimed horses from the city streets.

Fog, those old-time pea-soupers in which drivers could not see the horses at the end of their reins and street arabs with flaring torches guided pedestrians home for a few pence, often brought traffic in the towns to a complete standstill. Night-time driving was always full of perils, particularly in the countryside, as the road was only faintly illuminated by the weak glow of wax or composition candles in a pair of

METROPOLITAN
DRINKING FOUNTAIN & CATTLE TROUGH
ASSOCIATION

carriage lamps. Colza oil lamps gave a brighter light but also produced an abominable smell so that they were rarely used in private carriages. As a consequence, the state of the moon tended to govern night-time social life in the countryside, with dinner parties being held, whenever possible, when the moon was full. Even then, invitations had to be confined to those who lived within horse-and-carriage range, until more rural railway lines were built.[18]

In that age of free enterprise, everyone wanted to behave exactly as they liked on the roads. The first traffic signals were not introduced in London until 1868. At about the same time, the police started to have greater success in persuading drivers that it might be easier for everyone if they all kept to the left-hand side of the road; but many rich people continued to behave as if the roads existed for them alone. In Edwardian times, Sir Alexander Bruce, the Assistant Commissioner of the Metropolitan Police, was still complaining about "bad, careless or inconsiderate" drivers, who occupied "an unfair share of room, as can be seen by comparing the trail of vehicles leaving the Park with the closely-packed mass of mixed vehicles in the ordinary street". He suggested that driving licences might solve the problem, though he realized that private carriage owners would certainly object, and to exempt them and their servants would have been invidious.[19]

Carriage owners did have some legal privileges. Under a law passed in the reign of George III, cab drivers were obliged to give them priority, though few of them did so. Private carriages could also wait where they liked and as long as they liked without fear of prosecution unless the police could prove obstruction, which was often difficult when most magistrates were also carriage owners. Although cabs, vans and commercial carts had no such privileges, they often staked out their own claims by parking "two or three deep" to load or unload.[20] Many commercial vehicles were dangerously overloaded. Timber and coal carts were among the worst offenders with their loads sometimes rising up "fifteen feet high, with baskets up to the second floor windows, nearly".[21] Other carts had heavy iron girders and thirty-foot-long ladders protruding from them. Heavy goods vehicles slowed down the flow of traffic by hugging the crown of the road as the cambered sides were often greasy and slippery, because shopkeepers objected to the roads being sanded through fears that the sand might be blown on to their display of goods outside.[22] Builders also added to the congestion by claiming large areas of the pavements and the roads as gratuitous work yards, while many other streets were closed for days

(Left) *The Victorians provided some comforts for horses by building horse troughs all over London.*

at a time for repaving or repairing; the laying of gas and water pipes, telegraph wires, and pneumatic dispatch tubes; and the construction of sewers and tunnels.[23]

A few new roads were built in London to relieve the worst traffic congestion. The construction of Duncannon Street temporarily reduced the traffic jams at Charing Cross, while the building of New Oxford Street allowed traffic to flow more freely in High Holborn. But vested interests prevented any rational replanning of the capital's thoroughfares such as had occurred in Paris during the Second Empire when Baron Haussmann constructed the first network of wide handsome boulevards. London continued to seize up. Only 154 of the 913 streets, alleys and lanes in the City were wide enough to admit two or more lines of carriages.[24] As long ago as 1863, traffic in the City had reached saturation point, with 13,000 to 20,000 vehicles crossing, or trying to cross, London Bridge between the hours of 8 a.m. and 8 p.m. every working day, and 12,000 vehicles passing through Cheapside. In an earlier, more gentle, age it had been a common courtesy for the driver of a private carriage never to overtake that of a friend or an acquaintance; the problem in the succeeding overcrowded and more competitive age was much more frequently how to overtake anyone at all. More than a century ago, it was already far quicker to walk in Cheapside or Poultry than it was to travel in a vehicle.[25]

But it was generally far safer to fume silently or to curse openly in a traffic jam than it was to dismount, as one angry German visitor found to his alarm when he got out of his cab which was stuck in the middle of the traffic on London Bridge. "In wrath you now seize your purse, settle up and jump out of the carriage, intending to advance on foot if the worst comes to the worst. In reality, however, you feel at once how rashly your anger has led you to act. There you stand, hemmed in between two long lines of carriages and realize the impossibility of even reaching the footpath, so near and yet so far. Every movement of the carriage brings you into the greatest danger of falling under the wheels."[26]

It was, indeed, almost as dangerous to walk or to drive in Victorian city streets as it is today. In London, after allowance has been made for the increase in population, almost as many people were seriously injured in road accidents in 1872 as in 1972 and there were about half the number of deaths. As the Victorians did not go out nearly as much as people do today – hundreds of thousands of maidservants, for example, were confined to their houses week after week with only one short evening break every seven days – the real accident rate per

This photograph taken in the 1890s shows the great congestion in The Strand. Some other London streets were even more jammed with horse-drawn traffic during the rush hours.

road-user may have been even higher. In addition, there was widespread carnage among the horses. In bad weather, the streets resembled a knacker's yard more than a public thoroughfare: during the severe snowstorms in London in 1886, forty-nine horses died and another thousand were injured. The public concern over the slaughter of animals and human beings became so great that a Dangerous Driving Prevention Society was formed in 1889.[27]

People were crushed to death between carriage wheels; the pole of the vehicle behind broke through the back panels of a carriage injuring or killing some of the passengers; women hurled themselves screaming from their carriages as the horses bolted. Sir George Stephen remembered seeing a gentleman who was driving a phaeton steering his runaway horse into some iron railings in Cavendish Square to shatter its head.[28] During the day, London bobbies walked at their regulation speed of two-and-a-half miles an hour along the kerb so that they could jump out as quickly as possible into the road to stop any runaway horse.

Even in the wealthiest and the best regulated families, the chances of being injured in a road accident were very high. The Queen herself was involved in a number of accidents. Princess Marie Louise recalled how she was sitting in her room one day when a royal page came in and said breathlessly that Queen Victoria wanted to see her straight away:

> I leapt out to the corridor and found her half sitting and half lying in a little passage.
> "My dear, I have had a terrible accident."
> "Good heavens, what?" I said.
> Apparently the horse had shied and nearly upset the carriage and, in Grandmama's words, "Dear Frankie Clark (who succeeded John Brown) lifted me out of the carriage and, would you believe it, all my petticoats came undone."[29]

Another accident in which the Queen was involved was far more serious. In 1863 her carriage turned over on its side in the Highlands and she was thrown to the ground and was lucky to escape with relatively minor injuries.[30]

There was no effective insurance against road accidents until the Seventies when the Carriage Accident Insurance Company introduced a policy providing cover for damage to carriages and third-party liability, but insurance was not then compulsory. There was little danger of being convicted for causing a road accident. In Liverpool, for example, twenty-three people were killed and 486 injured in

(Left) Punch *was always indignantly opposed to the awkward carter who insisted on driving in the middle of the street.*

road accidents in 1872, but only thirteen people were fined and none imprisoned; in Manchester, where eighteen were killed and 231 injured, eight people were fined; and in Leeds, with ten deaths and thirty-five people injured, only one person was charged and fined.[31] People had to defend their own interests for themselves, which could often lead to prolonged and acrimonious correspondence between the parties involved.

The Earl of Radnor's coach was damaged in a collision with the Duke of Beaufort's cabriolet and, six months later, the earl sent off a bill for £42 1s., which included, rather impudently, a charge of £6 15s. for conveying the coach back by rail from Liverpool, where he had sent it to be repaired, and another £11 1s. for hiring a carriage while the coach was off the road. The duke was not particularly pleased to receive this large, belated demand, particularly as he considered himself to have been the main victim, and he sent off an indignant letter of protest to the Earl of Radnor:

> I was coming quietly out of my own Gateway in my Cabriolet, accompanied by one of my little girls, when your Coachman drove so suddenly across me, that I had the greatest Difficulty in saving my Horse from being seriously injured; had I been driving faster, he must inevitably have had his neck broken; as it was by turning short into Lord Sefton's gateway, he escaped with some Bruises and Abrasions of the Skin on the Head and Shoulders; the Harness was pulled and lightly injured, and the Shaft of the Cabriolet broken; and I thought myself fortunate to escape without further injury as, at one moment, I expected nothing short of Destruction both to myself and my little child.
>
> I certainly was not a little surprised when your Footman in rather an impertinent manner said he came to "insist on having my Card". I told him he need not fear my concealing my name as I should report the circumstance to you ...
>
> From that time, I heard no more of it except, as I understood, that you had discharged your Servant and till the Receipt of your letter, I certainly was under the impression that I was the *only* Sufferer from the Accident, as I must repeat that whatever Harm was done was occasioned by your Coachman, as *He* drove across *me*, and *not* I across Him ...

The correspondence dragged on, but after an exchange of several more letters, the duke became bored with his fellow-peer's persistence and paid the bill in full "as it really is not worth the trouble of writing so many letters".[32]

It was easier on the whole to accept road accidents with resignation and a stiff upper lip, which indicated aristocratic character in those times. Lord Grantley recalls how, as a young boy, he was being driven with his mother and sister along

Bond Street during the closing year of Victoria's reign when the horses bolted: "We careered along – Joan and myself yelling with terror; the coachman pulling desperately but ineffectively at the reins; the footman trying to pull too, but in some doubt as to whether it would be more prudent to jump from the box, and only deterred because we were travelling at a good thirty miles an hour. Through all this, Mother sat back immensely calm under her parasol, just as if she had been stuck to her seat, quite unmoved either by the imminent peril or the ominous swaying of the carriage. By some miracle we hit nothing; and when the coachman managed to pull up the horses by some means or other amid the politely murmured congratulations of the crowd which had gathered, Mother proceeded to scold everyone present in a majestic and terrifying voice.

"My sister and I were coldly rebuked for our craven screams; the coachman for letting his horses bolt; the footman for general incompetence and cowardice; and adjacent policeman for wasting her time by taking those copious notes in which the law always indulges on such occasions; and the crowd in general for gaping. Whereupon, disregarding the policeman's protests that he was still interested in the matter, my mother directed the carriage to proceed, and haughtily continued her shopping expedition in deadly silence."[33]

10

THE HORSELESS CARRIAGE

Throughout the nineteenth century, dozens of hopeful inventors tried to harness the forces of nature to a carriage in place of a horse. In 1823, Fordham of London designed an air carriage, driven by two cylinders of compressed air connected to a crankshaft, and a few years later, Col. Sir James Viney and George Pocock invented the *char volant*, a carriage pulled by kites and steered by parachutes, whose main drawback was that it could be used only in open treeless country when there was neither a gale nor a calm.[1] In the 1840s, *Punch* added its own prophetic and fanciful ideas to the solution of the problem of urban transport by advocating the construction of an underground railway, which was built some twenty years later, and an aerial omnibus, suspended from wires, which never was.

The most successful idea was the steam-driven carriage or omnibus. Steam was first used successfully as a means of propulsion on roads, not on rails. William Murdock, the inventor of gas lighting, built a successful model of a three-wheeled steam carriage between 1784 and 1786, and in 1802, the versatile Cornish engineer, Richard Trevithick and his cousin, Andrew Vivian, patented the first successful steam carriage. They brought it to London by sea and gave a demonstration on a site near Euston Square. Twenty or so other engineers and inventors also built steam carriages, including Julius Griffith, Sir Charles Dance, Sir Goldsworthy Gurney, Walter Hancock, and John Scott Russell. But in the early days of steam, the main encouragement and financial support came from far-sighted colliery owners who saw the possibilities of using powerful locomotives to haul their heavy tubs of coal along iron railroads which connected their pits to the staithes at sea and river ports. George Stephenson, a £100-a-year enginewright at Killingworth Colliery, built his first successful locomotive there in 1814 and within eight years had constructed locomotives and an eight-mile-long railway line at Hetton Colliery. In 1825, the thirty-seven-mile-long Stockton–Darlington line was

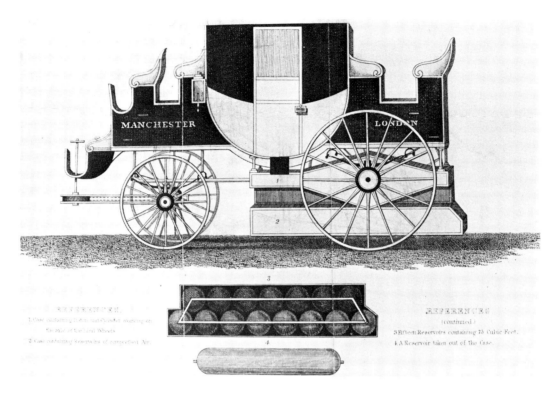

One of the early designs for a horseless carriage – Mann's Patent Locomotive Air Carriage. *It was driven by compressed air and its maximum range was claimed to be thirty-four miles.*

opened: its main purpose was to transport coal from Durham pits to the port of Stockton, but it also carried passengers. The success of railways was assured by the opening of the Liverpool–Manchester line in 1830.

Despite the great public interest in these developments on rail and road, both locomotives and steam carriages suffered at first from the "prejudices which always beset a new invention".[2] When the Liverpool and Manchester Railway Bill was being debated in the House of Commons in 1826, the M.P. for Ilchester, Sir Isaac Coffin, asked:

> How would any person like to have a railroad under his parlour window? ... What, he would like to know, was to be done with all those who had advanced money in making and repairing turnpike roads? What with those who may still wish to travel in their own or hired carriages, after the fashion of their forefathers? What was to become of coachmakers and harness-makers, coach-masters and coachmen, inn-

keepers, horse-breeders, and horse-dealers? Was the House aware of the smoke and noise, the hiss and whirl which locomotives engines passing at the rate of ten or twelve miles an hour, would occasion? Neither the cattle in the fields or grazing in the meadows could behold them without dismay.[3]

Although some lords with mineral interests supported the building of the railways, there were many reactionary members of the landed establishment who were opposed, fearing that the railways would introduce trespassing surveyors and gangs of filthy navvies into the quiet domains which they had dominated for so long, and bring poverty to the forage trade and fear into the hearts of their own, and their tenant-farmers' cattle and horses. Initially, some aristocrats refused to sell land to railway companies which wanted to build lines across their estates; but when they realized that many of the dire predictions of Sir Isaac Coffin were not being fulfilled and that the value of land near railway lines usually appreciated, their attitudes changed. Mr. J. Moss, a director of the Liverpool and Manchester Railway, told an inquiry in the 1830s that both the Earl of Derby and the Earl of Sefton had refused to sell land to his company, but that they had agreed to sell land to another of his companies a few years later for the construction of the London–Birmingham line.[4]

Steam carriages benefited by no such reversal of views. Railway companies built their permanent ways at their own expense; but steam carriages used existing turnpike roads, whose existence was already threatened by the new railways. The trustees of the turnpike roads claimed that steam carriages would damage the surface of their roads; but, in reality, they feared that their introduction would damage the forage trade, in which many trustees had a direct interest. To keep steam carriages off their roads, they started to charge excessive tolls. Sir Goldsworthy Gurney, who ran a steam-carriage service between Gloucester and Cheltenham four times a day between February and July, 1831, was forced to bring the service to an end because he could not afford to pay the tolls. He told the Select Committee on Steam Carriages in 1831 that his steam carriage would have had to pay £2 8s. on the Liverpool–Prescot Road against 4s. for a stagecoach; £1 7s. 1d. on the Bathgate Road against 5s.; £2 on the Ashburnham–Totnes Road against 3s.; and 12s. on the Teignmouth and Dawlish road against 2s.[5]

If excessive tolls failed to stop steam carriages, the trustees sometimes resorted to sabotage. John Scott Russell opened a daily service with four, wooden-wheeled steam carriages between Glasgow and Paisley while he was working as a shipyard manager at Greenock in 1830. He told a select committee that the trustees had

An illustration from Boy's Own Paper *of 1896. The original caption read: "A Vision of the Happy Auto-motor Days to Come."*

"laid down eighteen inches deep of fresh broken granite on all the most difficult parts of the road, those going uphill, and they also laid down a considerable tract at the tollgate nearest Glasgow, so deep that they had to cut off the whole bottom of the gates before they could get them to close and open upon this relay of stones, and they succeeded in driving everybody off the road except us, for there was another way to Paisley, only a good deal roundabout. We determined we would not be driven off the road, and we continued our traffic, but we had to have one new set of wheels every day, and we had a large establishment making new wheels, which we put on every morning. At last one wheel broke down at 4 o'clock, before it was time to go home and have a new one, and the breaking down of that wheel let the boot fall to the ground, and the ground tore the bottom off the boiler and produced an explosion which injured many passengers." Several of the passengers died later from their wounds. Russell had no doubts about the reason for this sabotage: "We

127

were going to displace horses, and damage the great agricultural interest, and therefore our friends who were agriculturists determined to put our carriage down."[6]

Steam carriages aroused opposition from other pressure groups, too. Walter Hancock, of Stratford, operated some of the most successful services in London with his *Era, Autopsy* and *Automaton*. One Victorian reporter who accompanied the *Era* on its first journey from Moorfields to Paddington in 1834 at an average speed of 12 m.p.h. reported enthusiastically:

> The noise is not greater than that of a common omnibus; indeed so trifling is it, or the peculiarity of the appearance of the machine altogether, that horses meeting it hardly appeared in the least degree frightened. There is neither smoke nor disagreeable smell of any kind; the motion is not so great as in a coach; and, in short, as a conveyance, it is fully as comfortable as the best-constructed stage-coach ... On the whole, the result of the first day's trip has been such as cannot leave a doubt upon the mind as to the ultimate success of steam-carriages upon common roads.[7]

But horse-drawn omnibus proprietors petitioned parliament against the use of Hancock's steam carriages on the roads, and after a few years he gave up his experiments.

There seems little doubt that steam carriages could have provided an acceptable alternative to horse-drawn transport in the cities and towns. Although early steam carriages, like railway locomotives, had their teething troubles, all the parliamentary select committees which investigated them in Victorian times gave favourable reports. The very first committee said in 1831 that steam carriages could ascend and descend hills safely, that they were "perfectly safe" for passengers, that they caused less wear and tear on roads than coaches and horses, and that they "will become a speedier and cheaper mode of conveyance than carriages drawn by horses".[8] But vested interests drove them off the roads.

Steam locomotives continued to be used mainly in agriculture, particularly for threshing. There was some revival of interest in steam carriages in the Sixties by which time many of the turnpike trusts had gone into liquidation; but the railway

(Right above) *Three of the steam carriages built by Walter Hancock –* The Autopsy, Era *and* Infant.

(Right below) *Horse-drawn Transport at Hyde Park Corner – a painting by Herbert Marshall.*

lobby in parliament proved to be no less of a formidable enemy of steam carriages. (Over one-third of M.P.s were directors or managers of railway companies.) In 1865, the infamous Locomotive Act was passed, which effectively prevented further experiments with mechanically-propelled vehicles on the roads, leaving them clear for a later take-over by Continental motor-cars. Clause after clause imposed severe restrictions on "every locomotive propelled by Steam or other than Animal Power on any Turnpike Road or public Highway.

> Firstly, at least Three Persons shall be employed to drive or conduct such Locomotive, and if more than Two Wagons or Carriages be attached thereto, an additional Person shall be employed, who shall take charge of such Wagons or Carriages: Secondly, one of such Persons, while any Locomotive is in Motion, shall precede such Locomotive on Foot by not less than Sixty Yards, and shall carry a Red Flag constantly displayed, and shall warn Riders and Drivers of Horses of the Approach of such Locomotives, and shall signal the Driver thereof when it shall be necessary to stop, and shall assist Horses and Carriages drawn by Horses, passing the same ... Fourthly, the Whistle of such Locomotive shall not be sounded for any purpose whatever ...
> Fifthly, every such Locomotive shall be instantly stopped, on the Person preceding the same, or any other Person with a Horse, or a Carriage drawn by horse, putting up his Hand as a Signal."

Steam carriages were also restricted to a speed of 4 m.p.h. in the countryside and 2 m.p.h. in towns.

That the red flag clause was nothing but a prejudiced piece of railway-lobby legislation designed to cripple steam carriages was nicely demonstrated by Mr. John Forbes White, an Aberdeen miller who used three road locomotives. He told the Select Committee on Locomotive Engines on Roads in 1873:

> If a man goes forward with a flag if a horse is frightened, waving the flag only makes the horse more frightened; besides, if a man holds a flag in his hand, his right hand is powerless, and he cannot assist when his assistance would be useful, say in the case of a restive horse.[9]

A new Act of 1878 made no mention of the red flag, though some local

(Left above) *Horse-drawn trams and hansoms near St. Pancras, with smoke and fog.*

(Left below) *Some of the first motor cabs which were soon to banish hansom cabs entirely from the London streets.*

authorities continued to insist on its use; but a man had to walk at least twenty yards in front of any road locomotive and owners were obliged to buy a £10 licence for each county in which the vehicle was used. The obligation to have a look-out man was not abolished until 1896, when the maximum speed limit was also raised to 14 m.p.h., though many local authorities fixed it at 12 m.p.h. under their by-laws. By the time these restrictions on road transport had been abolished, Continental competitors had gained a great lead. In Germany, Gottlieb Daimler and Karl Benz had both produced a four-wheeled motor-car by 1886, and in France, by the Nineties, Peugeot and Renault had incorporated many modern features in their cars. Léon Serpollet had brought the steam car to such a state of perfection that he gained the world speed record of just over 75 m.p.h. in 1902.

It was not that the British lacked inventiveness. On January 10, 1863, the first underground railway in the world, the Metropolitan Railway, was opened from Paddington to Farringdon Street, and in 1890 the first electric Tube trains started running under the Thames from King William Street to Stockwell. In 1885, Edward Butler of Newbury, Berkshire, exhibited a petrol-driven tricycle at the International Inventions Exhibition in London in the same year as Benz produced his first tricycle. In that year, too, J. K. Starley, of Coventry, invented the first practical safety bicycle with a chain-driven rear wheel. In 1888, John Boyd Dunlop, a Scottish veterinary surgeon, patented his pneumatic tyre and in the same year Magnus Volk, the managing director of the Brighton Electric Railway, produced an electric dog cart, powered by accumulators which gave a six-hour drive. Frederick Lanchester built his first motor-car in 1895 and six years later started manufacturing a ten-horsepower car of advanced design with automatic lubrication and an air-cooled engine.

But, too often, inventors lacked encouragement or support, or came up against the stubborn conservative opposition of the establishment. Aristocrats opposed the London underground railways fearing that the noise and vibration might damage their vast properties in the capital and disturb their tenants and thus reduce their own rent roll, which provoked *Punch* to remind them: "London is not a Cathedral Close, or a Stagnant Country Conservative Town; but a busy hive of four millions of people, who have to push, rush, sweat and struggle to pay rent and taxes, and get a living."[10] The judges at the International Inventions Exhibition were so unimpressed by Butler's tricycle that they didn't even give him an award. Frederick Lanchester failed to receive the recognition he deserved until just before his death in 1946. The first cyclists were so unpopular because it was feared that they would frighten horses that they were known as "cads on castors", though

The final years of the horse in Cheapside which was soon to be filled with very different kinds of vehicles.

cycling became more popular later among the upper and the middle classes particularly after the Prince of Wales took to wheels. Gwen Raverat, recalling her Cambridge childhood, wrote: "Bicycles gradually became the chief vehicles for ladies paying calls. They would even tuck up their trains and ride out to dinner on them. One summer evening my parents rode ten miles to dine at Six Mile Bottom; their evening clothes were carried in cases on the handlebars; for, of course, you couldn't possibly dine without dressing."[11]

By Edwardian times there was an extraordinary variety of vehicles on the roads, including electric cars and trams, horse-drawn omnibuses, steam-driven lorries, petrol-driven motor-cars, bicycles and all the old horse-drawn vehicles from barouches to baker's vans. Of the 24,411 vehicles which passed along Piccadilly in one day in May, 1903, 1,066 were two-wheeled carts, 7,755 were two-wheeled carriages and hansom cabs, 3,501 were four-wheeled carts and wagons, 3,994 were four-wheeled carriages and cabs, 6,101 were buses, 1,522 were cycles, 392 were motor-cars and 89 were commercial vans.[12] Many of the upper and the middle classes continued to ride in carriages and to cling obstinately to their belief that this form of transport would "persist, at any rate, for the next century or two."[13] Tillings still owned 7,000 horses (and twenty motor buses) in 1905 and had at least 10,000 horses out on hire for the coronation of George V in 1911.[14] But as it became increasingly obvious that the horse and carriage was doomed, the more enterprising tradesmen and manufacturers started to diversify their interests into the new horseless carriage age. Horse dealers and jobmasters started to hire out petrol landaulettes and electric cars; coachmakers began to build car bodies; some coachmen retrained as chauffeurs.

Changes occurred even more rapidly and dramatically in public transport. Before the First World War, the new double-decker buses and motor cabs had driven most horse-drawn omnibuses and hansom cabs off the roads. Hansom cab drivers found it even more difficult to make a living than it had ever been. Many of their horses were so undernourished and so little used that even when a customer came along, the horse was "too stiff to move at anything above a snail's pace".[15] In 1912, a Horses' and Drivers' Aid Committee was formed "to equip and provide suitable horse-drawn vehicles for those cab drivers too old to learn to drive motors" and to give them a guaranteed wage of £1 a week. But many cabbies gave up the unequal struggle like fifty-eight-year-old William Henry Upton, of Kingston, Surrey, who committed suicide by jumping into the Thames. In a letter left for his wife, he wrote: "Cab work has broken my heart. It is no good. I know it will be starvation for the next six months. Was out for twelve hours on Sunday for 1s. 3d. I can't stand it any longer."[16] By 1914 there were only just over 200 hansom cabs in London compared with 7,500 in 1903.

The horse-drawn vehicle survived the First World War. A few London doctors continued to job horses up to about 1923 and ten years later, in the whole country, there were still twenty thousand or so private carriages. Brewer's drays, milk floats, coal carts, railway delivery vans, rag and bone men's carts continued to be seen in the streets, but the great days of the horse and carriage had passed. After many thousands of years of arduous, if not always entirely willing, service, the horse as a means of transport had finally succumbed to the internal combustion machine.

11

EPILOGUE

Although the last days of the horse and carriage age remain well within living memory, it has been submerged so completely by history that the rare survivals have a curiously antique air. A few coaches and carriages are preserved in museums throughout the country and others are sometimes discovered rotting in some country barn, when, after restoration, they can be sold for many thousands of pounds on the private collectors' market. Our language still retains vestigial traces of that vanished age so that we speak of "driving" a car or a train, of railway coaches, and of the booking office, where in former times the names of stagecoach passengers were entered in a book. The British Driving Society, founded in 1954, has revived interest in coaches and carriages and the mysteries of real driving. And every year, thousands of tourists visit the Royal Mews in London to catch a last whiff of the horse and carriage age. The Royal Mews is more than a superlative museum: the royal broughams are still employed every day to carry official despatches and most of the thirty other carriages are used from time to time.

The Royal Mews is the most appropriate memorial, the transcendent example, of the horse and carriage age, for, in spite of middle-class incursions, the coach and the carriage were never suitable vehicles for democratic times, needing space and leisure which were the prerogatives of the monarchy and the aristocracy. The horse and carriage age has been suffused by our nostalgia in a roseate glow which softens the harsher outlines of existential reality.

REFERENCES

(Place of publication is London if not stated. P.P. = Parliamentary Papers)

The Horse and Carriage Age
1. Elliott O'Donnell (ed.) *Mrs. E. M. Ward's Reminiscences*, Pitman, 1911, p. 67
2. John Forster, *The Life of Charles Dickens*, Chapman and Hall, 1873–4, Vol. II, p. 243
3. Athol Maudslay, *Highways and Horses*, Chapman and Hall, 1888, p. 72
4. John R. Kellett, *The Impact of Railways on Victorian Cities*, Routledge, 1969, p. 319
5. W. J. Gordon, *The Horse World of London*, Leisure Hour, 1891, Vol. 41, p. 389
6. Henry Mayhew, *London Labour and the London Poor*, Griffin, 1861, Vol. II, p. 217
7. *Everybody's Carriage Stops the Way*, Chamber's Journal, London and Edinburgh, October 20, 1866, pp. 659–60
8. Ishbel, Marchioness of Aberdeen, *The musings of a Scottish Granny*, Heath Cranton, 1936, p. 21
9. Lady Clodagh Anson, *Victorian Days*, Richard Press, 1957, p. 49
10. Mrs. C. E. Humphry, *Manners for Men*, Bowden, 1898, pp. 32, 46
11. Rev. J. G. Wood, *Horse and Man*, Longmans, 1885, p. 219
12. Horace Smith, *A Horseman through Six Reigns*, Odhams, 1955, p. 56
13. George Augustus Sala, *Carriage People*, Belgravia, 1875, Vol. 26, p. 474

Aristocratic Splendour
1. John Hollingshead, *Miscellanies*, Tinsley, 1874, Vol. 11, p. 350
2. Gordon op. cit. p. 320
3. *Illustrated London News*, January 14, 1854
4. Mrs. Newton Crosland, *Landmarks of a Literary Life*, Sampson Low, Marston, 1893, p. 98
5. Marchioness of Bath, *Before the Sunset Fades*, Longleat Estate Co., Longleat, 1951, p. 12
6. Goodwood Archives, E. 5470, West Sussex Record Office, Chichester
7. *Rambles Round Nottingham*, Simpkin Marshall, 1856, Vol. I, pp. 103–4
8. Robert Kerr, *The Gentleman's House*, Murray, 1871, p. 257
9. Benjamin Moran, *The Footpath and Highway*, Lippincott, Philadelphia, USA, 1853, p. 61
10. S. Sidney, *The Book of the Horse*, Cassell, 1881, p. 246
11. Count Charles Frederick Vitzthum, *St. Petersburg and London in the Years 1852–64*, Longmans, 1887, Vol. I, p. 230
12. Smith op. cit. p. 54
13. Gordon op. cit. p. 391
14. Earl of Onslow, *The Carriage Horse*, in the Duke of Beaufort (ed.) Driving, Longmans, 1889, p. 59

15. Wood op. cit. pp. 268–73
16. Stephen Harding Terry, *The Crime of Docking Horses*, RSPCA, n.d. p. 11
17. *Rambles Round Nottingham*, loc. cit.
18. Emma Sophia, Countess Brownlow, *The Eve of Victorianism*, Murray, 1940, p. 144
19. Anson op. cit. p. 44
20. Sala op. cit. p. 475
21. Oliver Wendell Holmes, *Our Hundred Days in Europe*, Sampson Low, Marston, 1892, p. 67
22. Elizabeth Davis Bancroft, *Letters from England*, Smith Elder, 1904, p. 64
23. Sir Walter Gilbey, *Modern Carriages*, Vinton, 1905, p. 18
24. Sidney op. cit. p. 533
25. Gervas Huxley, *Victorian Duke*, Oxford University Press, 1967, p. 138
26. Bath, loc. cit.
27. Frederick John Gorst (with Beth Andrews) *Of Carriages and Kings*, W. H. Allen, 1956, pp. 130–1
28. Mary Paley Marshall, *What I Remember*, Cambridge University Press, 1947, p. 3
29. Goodwood Estate Archives op. cit. 1096
30. Marylian Watney, *The Elegant Carriage*, J. A. Allen, 1961, p. 51
31. Ashburnham MSS, 2657, East Sussex Record Office, Lewes
32. Ibid, 1814
33. Ibid, 2668
34. Alfred E. T. Watson, *The Cost of a Carriage*, in Beaufort op. cit. p. 114
35. Goodwood Archives op. cit. E. 5470
36. *Select Committee on Horses*, P.P. Vol. XIV, Q 857, 860

Life in Mews and Stables

1. F. H. W. Sheppard (ed.) *Survey of London*, The Museums Area of South Kensington and Westminster, Greater London Council, 1975, p. 263
2. Mitford Archives, 2147, West Sussex Record Office
3. Sidney op. cit. pp. 498–9
4. Byng Giraud, *Stable Building and Stable Fitting*, Batsford, 1891, p. 7
5. Onslow op. cit. p. 75
6. Mayhew op. cit. Vol. II, pp. 233–4
7. Interview with Mr. R. Barley
8. Mayhew op. cit. Vol. II, p. 554
9. Ernest H. Shephard, *Drawn from Memory*, Methuen, 1957, p. 139
10. Sir George Stephen, *The Groom*, Knight, 1840, p. 28
11. Ibid, p. 39
12. Ibid, pp. 37–8
13. *The Servants' Practical Guide*, Warne n.d. p. 186
14. Charles S. Pelham-Clinton, *The Stables of the Queen of England*, Cosmopolitan, New York, 1889, Vol. VIII, p. 19
15. Samuel and Sarah Adams, *The Complete Servant*, Knight and Lacey, 1825, p. 375
16. Maudslay op. cit. p. 450
17. S. and S. Adams op. cit. p. 372
18. Beaufort op. cit. pp. 16, 3
19. Maudslay op. cit. p. 318
20. Sir George Stephen, *The Groom* op. cit. p. 24
21. Wood op. cit. pp. 255–6
22. Lord William Pitt Lennox, *Coaching*, Hurst and Blackett, 1876, p. 248
23. Henry White, *The Record of my Life*, Cheltenham, 1889, p. 149
24. Wood op. cit. p. 263

25. A Stud Groom, *The Management and Treatment of the Horse*, London Literary Society, 1882, p. 34
26. Eric Horne, *What the Butler Winked At*, Laurie, n.d. pp. 77–8
27. William Bridges Adams, *English Pleasure Carriages*, Adams and Dart, Bath, 1971, pp. 221–3
28. Eric Horne, *More Winks*, Laurie, 1932, p. 79
29. Quoted in Ralph Straus, *Carriages and Coaches*, Martin Secker, 1912, p. 277
30. A. L. Kennedy, *Salisbury*, Murray, 1953, p. 241
31. John Jervis, *The Horse and Carriage Keeper's Oracle*, Colburn, 1827, p. 94; W. B. Adams op. cit. p. 254
32. Arthur W. Moss, *Valiant Crusade*, Cassell, 1961, p. 99
33. Jervis op. cit. p. 102
34. *Medical Times*, July 26, 1851

The Gig Set
1. Sidney op. cit. p. 3
2. Humphrey op. cit. p. 30
3. Ibid, p. 98
4. Ibid, p. 29
5. A Member of the Aristocracy, *Manners and Tone of Good Society*, Warne, n.d. p. 184
6. Ibid, p. 183
7. Idem
8. Lady Colin Campbell (ed.) *Etiquette of Good Society*, Cassell, 1911, p. 190
9. Richard Jeffries, *Hodge and his Masters*, MacGibbon and Kee, 1966, Vol. I, p. 95
10. J. R. Planché, *Recollections and Reflections*, Tinsley, 1872, Vol. I, p. 29
11. Edith Sitwell, *English Eccentrics*, Arrow, 1960, p. 141
12. Gorst op. cit. p. 61
13. Kellett op. cit. pp. 355–61
14. *Carriages and Their Changes, All the Year Round*, January 13, 1866, p. 13
15. Hollingshead, op. cit. p. 148
16. Sidney op. cit. p. 526
17. Mrs. C. S. Peel, *Life's Enchanted Cup*, John Lane, 1933, p. 95
18. A Member of the Aristocracy op. cit. p. 184
19. Sala op. cit. p. 474
20. Watson op. cit. pp. 110–11
21. Ibid, p. 107; Sidney op. cit. p. 506
22. Select Committee on Highway Acts, P.P. 1881, Vol. X, Q 64
23. Returns Relating to Stage Carriages, P.P. 1865, Vol. XXXI, passim.
24. Jervis op. cit. p. 18
25. Hollingshead, op. cit. p. 150
26. Edward Corbett, *An Old Coachman's Chatter*, Bentley, 1890, p. 88
27. Sir George Stephen, *Caveat Emptor, The Adventures of a Gentleman in Search of a Horse*, Sanders and Otley, 1836, p. 140
28. A Stud Groom op. cit. p. 33
29. Joseph Arch, *Autobiography*, MacGibbon and Kee, 1966, p. 30
30. White op. cit. pp. 48, 59
31. Marshall op. cit. p. 4
32. George Henry Hewit Oliphant, *The Law of the Horse*, Sweet, 1854, pp. 337–8
33. RSPCA Annual Report, 1862–3, RSPCA, 1864, p. 66
34. *The Times*, November 28, 1866
35. *Evening Star*, August 15, 1864
36. RSPCA Annual Report, 1856, pp. 66–8

37. Ibid, 1861, pp. 212–4

Horse Dealers and Copers

1. Sidney op. cit. p. 240; F. P. G. Guizot, *Memoirs of Sir Robert Peel*, Bentley, 1857, pp. 349–51
2. Col. F. Fitzwygram, *Horses and Stables*, Longmans, 1869, p. 558
3. Screws, *The New Monthly Magazine*, Colburn, 1841, Vol. 62, p. 457
4. Ibid, p. 462
5. Onslow op. cit. p. 60
6. Stephen, *Caveat* op. cit. pp. 144–6
7. Oliphant op. cit. pp. 55 et seq.
8. Committee on Horses op. cit. Q 862
9. Cowdray Archives, 1906, (10), (11), West Sussex Record Office
10. Smith op. cit. pp. 61–2
11. Ibid, p. 120
12. "Thormanby", *The Horse and his Rider*, Chatto and Windus, 1888, pp. 187–8
13. Sidney op. cit. p. 184
14. Nimrod, *Memoirs of the late John Mytton*, Ackermann, 1837, p. 22
15. Oxford University and City Herald, April 29, 1826
16. Committee on Horses op. cit. Q 74
17. Sir Walter Gilbey, *The Harness Horse*, Vinton, 1898, p. 20
18. Charles Knight (ed.) *London, Virtue*, Vol. VI, p. 351

Carriages – for Sale or Hire

1. Quoted in Maudslay op. cit. p. 316
2. Lennox op. cit. p. 249
3. J. Phillipson, *Art and Craft of Coachbuilding*, Bell, 1897, p. 130
4. Ibid, p. 2
5. *Carriages and their Changes*, op. cit. p. 14
6. Brian Smith, *Windovers and Coachmaking in Huntingdon*, Longsands Museum Bulletin, Huntingdon, 1976, n.p.
7. Francis W. Steer, *Heraldic Coach Panels*, Sussex County Magazine, Eastbourne, Vol. XXIX, p. 262
8. Duke of Manchester Archives, DDM 20A/8, Huntingdon Record Office
9. Philipson op. cit. pp. 112–3
10. Hugh McCausland, *The English Carriage*, Batchworth Press, 1948, p. 108
11. Brian Smith loc. cit.
12. *The Hampshire Advertiser and Southampton Times*, March 26, 1938
13. Harold Nockolds (ed.) *The Coachmakers*, Allen, 1977, p. 111
14. H. Smith op. cit. pp. 52–3
15. Philipson op. cit. p. 180
16. Gilbey, *Modern Carriages*, op. cit. p. 70
17. Manchester Archives loc. cit.
18. Pleydell-Bouverie Papers, C.10, 1–12, Berkshire Record Office, Reading
19. Manchester Archives loc. cit.
20. *Our Carriage Horses, All the Year Round*, February 10, 1866, p. 112

Jobmasters

1. John Tilling, *Kings of the Highway*, Hutchinson, 1957, p. 57
2. Dick Hunt, *Bygones*, Baxter, Lewes, 1948, p. 28
3. Committee on Horses op. cit. Q 1–7

4. Tilling op. cit. p. 45
5. Interview with Mr. E. H. August
6. Tilling op. cit. pp. 35, 107
7. Gordon op. cit. p. 390
8. Hunt op. cit. pp. 31–2
9. Rambles Round Nottingham op. cit. pp. 263–6

Cabbies and Cads
1. Vitzthum op. cit. Vol. I, pp. 228–9
2. Charles Dickens, *Sketches by Boz*, Nelson, 1899, p. 51
3. Select Committee on London Traffic Regulations, P.P. 1863, Vol. X, p. 27
4. Kellett op. cit. p. 370
5. Peel op. cit. p. 95
6. G. C. Dickinson, *The Development of Suburban Road Passenger Transport in Leeds, 1840–95*, Journal of Transport History, Leicester University Press, 1960, Vol. IV, pp. 217, 220–1
7. Hunt op. cit. p. 29
8. Mayhew op. cit. Vol. II, p. 360
9. Henry Angelo, *Reminiscences*, Colburn and Bentley, 1830, Vol. II, p. 80
10. Dickens op. cit. p. 80
11. Lennox op. cit. p. 287
12. Henry Charles Moore, *Omnibuses and Cabs*, Chapman and Hall, 1902, p. 240
13. Ibid, pp. 235–6
14. *Punch*, 1851, Vol. 21, p. 173
15. Royal Commission on London Traffic, P.P. 1905, Vol. II, Q 17239
16. Ibid, Q 17287
17. Mayhew op. cit. Vol. III, pp. 362–3
18. Morning Herald, May 17, 1864
19. RSPCA Annual Report, 1850, pp. 91–2
20. Ibid, 1856, p. 10
21. Committee on Horses op. cit. Q 2899–2908; Fitzwygram op. cit. p. 7
22. Charles Booth (ed.) *Life and Labour of the People in London*, Macmillan, 1896, Vol. VII, p. 302
23. J. M. Walker, *Wages Accounts*, 1891–2, Archives Department, Leeds City Library
24. Moore op. cit. pp. 164–78
25. Peel, op. cit. p. 95
26. Humphry op. cit. p. 39
27. G. A. Sekon, *Locomotion in Victorian London*, Oxford University Press, 1938, p. 33
28. Ibid, pp. 29–30
29. Mayhew op. cit. Vol. III, p. 354
30. *Punch*, 1847, Vol. 13, p. 83
31. Booth op. cit. pp. 311–3
32. Charles Manby Smith, *Curiosities of London Life*, Cash, 1853, p. 138
33. Tilling op. cit. p. 59
34. Gordon op. cit. pp. 533–4
35. Tilling op. cit. p. 63

Perils of the Roads
1. Maudslay op. cit. pp. 66–7
2. RSPCA Annual Report 1865, p. 21
3. *Punch*, 1868, Vol. 54, p. 67
4. Frederick A. Paget, *Report on Steam Road Rolling*, Judd and Glass, 1870, pp. 1–2
5. *Punch*, 1868, Vol. 54, p. 33

6. Paget op. cit. p. 21
7. Mayhew op. cit. Vol. II, p. 217
8. Maudslay op. cit. p. 68
9. Sir Henry Thomson, *Motor Cars and Health*, in Alfred C. Harmsworth (ed.) Motors and Motor Driving, Longmans, 1902, p. 78
10. F. M. L. Thompson, *Victorian England*; The Horse Drawn Society, Bedford College, University of London, 1970, p. 10
11. Gordon op. cit. pp. 249–50
12. William Haywood, *Report on Disposal of Refuse*, 1881, pp. 10–21
13. Ibid, p. 32
14. Returns on Paupers Employed in Cleansing the Streets of the Metropolis, P.P. 1856, Vol. XLIX, pp. 423–4
15. First Report on State of Large Towns, P.P., 1844, Vol. XVII, pp. 732–7
16. Mayhew op. cit. Vol. II, p. 529
17. William Haywood, *Report on Accidents to Horses*, Skipper and East, 1873, p. 35
18. Mrs. C. S. Peel, *A Hundred Wonderful Years*, Cassell, 1926, pp. 13, 119
19. Royal Commission on London Traffic op. cit. Appendix 13, p. 335
20. Committee on Traffic Regulations op. cit. p. 9
21. Ibid, p. 14
22. Commission on London Traffic op. cit. p. 328
23. Hollingshead op. cit. p. 322
24. *Chambers Journal* loc. cit.
25. Committee on Traffic Regulations op. cit. pp. 13–4
26. T. Fontane, *Journeys to England in Victoria's Early Days*, Massie, 1939, p. 78
27. Moss op. cit. p. 91
28. Stephen, *The Groom*, op. cit. p. 13
29. Princess Marie Louise, *My Memories of Six Reigns*, Penguin, Harmondsworth, 1959, p. 124
30. David Duff (ed.) *Victoria in the Highlands*, Muller, 1968, pp. 202–3
31. Carriage Accidents, P.P. 1873, Vol. LIII, p. 459
32. Pleydell-Bouverie Papers loc. cit.
33. Lord Grantley, *Silver Spoon* (ed. Mary and Alan Wood) Hutchinson, 1954, pp. 23–4

The Horseless Carriage
1. Thomas A. Croal, *A Book about Travelling*, Nimmo, 1877, pp. 129, 132
2. Report of Select Committee on Steam Carriages, P.P. 1831, Vol. VIII, p. 4
3. Samuel Smiles, *Lives of the Engineers*, Murray, 1862, Vol. III, p. 218
4. Nicholas Wilcox Cundy, *Inland Transit*, Herbert, 1833, p. 138
5. Committee on Steam Carriages op. cit. pp. 7–8
6. Select Committee on Locomotive Engines on Roads, P.P. 1873, Vol. XVI, Q 3207–9
7. *Morning Chronicle*, August 19, 1834
8. Select Committee on Steam Carriages op. cit. p. 14
9. Select Committee on Locomotive Engines op. cit. Q 486
10. *Punch*, 1882, Vol. 82, p. 286
11. Gwen Raverat, *Period Piece, A Cambridge Childhood*, Faber, 1952, pp. 85–6
12. Royal Commission on London Traffic op. cit. p. 446
13. Straus op. cit. p. 283
14. Tilling op. cit. pp. 107–8
15. Charles Reinhardt, Old Friends in Hard Times, The Horses' and Drivers' Aid Committee, n.d. p. 33
16. *Daily Express*, November 18, 1912

ILLUSTRATION ACKNOWLEDGEMENTS

The Book of the Horse by S. Sidney 9, 15, 21, 31, 41, 70, opp. 80 above; *Boys Own Paper* 127; *K. Fletcher* 125, opp. 128 above; *Glasgow Museum of Transport* 29, opp. 32 above and below, opp. 33 above and below; *Gunnersbury Park Museum* opp. 48 above and below; *Gwynedd Archives Service* 52, 88; *Hull Transport Museum* 26, 84; *London Transport Executive* 107, 131; *Mansell Collection* title page, 11, opp. 16 above, 46, 51, 56–7, 95; *Mary Evans Picture Library* 34, 43, opp. 49, opp. 65 above and below, 67, 82, 105; *The Museum of London* 78, 99, 102, 108, opp. 128 below, opp. 129 above and below; *Museum of Technology, Leicester* 61; *Paul Popper Ltd.* half-title page, 6, 12, opp. 17, 18, 38, opp. 96 above and below, 119; *Punch* 101, 114, 120; *Royal Society for the Prevention of Cruelty to Animals* opp. 112, 116; *The William Salt Library, Stafford* 92; *Crown Copyright – Science Museum, London* opp. 97 above; *M. A. Smith* 14; *Sotheby Parke Bernet & Co.* opp. 113 above and below; *F. Staff* 74, opp. 97 below; *J. Tilling* 86, 91, 110; *Victoria & Albert Museum – Crown Copyright* 24–5

INDEX

Figures in bold relate to illustrations

142